婺文化双语阅读系列　　　　　双语版

婺宝传奇

李慧　徐进 ◎ 编著

Appreciating Cultural Relics
in Jinhua Museums

上海财经大学出版社

本书由上海财经大学浙江学院发展基金与金华市博物馆共同资助出版

图书在版编目(CIP)数据

婺宝传奇:汉英对照/李慧,徐进编著.—上海:
上海财经大学出版社,2023.2
(婺文化双语阅读系列)
ISBN 978-7-5642-3989-3/F.3989

Ⅰ.①婺… Ⅱ.①李… ②徐… Ⅲ.①文物–介绍–金华–汉、英 Ⅳ.①K872.553

中国版本图书馆CIP数据核字(2022)第103050号

责任编辑　肖　蕾
书籍设计　张克瑶

婺宝传奇(双语版)

著　作　者：李　慧　徐　进　编著
出版发行：上海财经大学出版社有限公司
地　　址：上海市中山北一路369号(邮编200083)
网　　址：http://www.sufep.com
经　　销：全国新华书店
印刷装订：广东虎彩云印刷有限公司
开　　本：710 mm×1000 mm　1/16
印　　张：16.75
字　　数：246千字
版　　次：2023年2月第1版
印　　次：2023年2月第1次印刷
定　　价：98.00元

编审委员会

主 任

徐 卫　徐玉书

副主任

李 慧　朱 艳　徐 进　王明照

成 员

（按姓氏笔画排序）

王 芳	王永平	王诀思	王翔宇	韦杏雨	叶丽芳	叶睿静
吕沆泽	朱江平	朱 颖	江凌云	汤 煊	许 倩	应雨桦
陈 超	陈诗琪	周 凯	周铖涛	金言睿	金弦和	郑建明
祝碧莲	徐关元	徐浠静	曹艳梅	梁 妍	傅毅强	傅燕芳
童小婉	蔡 蕾	燕牧鹤				

编写委员会

主　编

李　慧　徐　进

副主编

许　倩　周　凯　朱　颖

编　委

王　芳	王永平	王诀思	王翔宇	韦杏雨	叶丽芳	叶睿静
叶剑韬	吕沅泽	朱江平	江凌云	汤　煊	吴国清	应雨桦
陈　超	陈诗琪	周铖涛	金言睿	金弦和	郑　静	郑建明
祝碧莲	徐关元	徐浠静	曹艳梅	梁　妍	彭昶虹	傅毅强
傅燕芳	童小婉	蔡　蕾	管欣怡	滕仲元	潘春艳	燕牧鹤

校　对

Nadiiev Artur　刘正波　朱雨晗

【前言】

馆校合作，是博物馆向外界传播文物知识、弘扬民族文化、增强文化自信的有效途径之一。开馆至今，金华市博物馆相继与多所院校达成了馆校合作意向。其中，上海财经大学浙江学院是首个与博物馆开展馆校合作的院校。

金华市博物馆与上海财经大学浙江学院自2015年9月开启馆校合作的序幕以来，已携手走过了7年。期间，馆校合作内容丰富、形式多样，博物馆每年策划课程、开发宣教、走进校园，为学院师生充实博物馆知识提供学术支撑。上海财经大学浙江学院师生积极参与博物馆志愿者服务活动、主动参与博物馆讲解稿英译、配合开展针对外宾的讲解，发挥出学院的专业优势。同时，多年的馆校合作也结出丰硕的成果，2019年双方合作出版了第一部馆校合作图书——《金华市博物馆实用英语》，取得了良好的社会反响。

2020年，为深入贯彻党中央、国务院关于博物馆及文物工作的系列指示精神，提升文物传播力、影响力，经研究，馆校双方拟合作编辑出版婺文化双语（中、英文）读本——《婺宝传奇》。全书共分为三部分，第一部分介绍金华市博物馆馆藏精品，内容涵盖陶瓷器、青铜器、玉器、金银器、书画精品；第二部分介绍金华下辖各县市博物馆的馆藏精品，涉及兰溪、义乌、东阳、永康、武义、浦江、磐安等县市；第三部分是难字阐析，围绕金华市博物馆八婺古韵、神奇大地、乡土民风、百工之乡四个基本陈列展厅的陈列展览展开。全书内容全面、资料翔实，不仅具有专业、权威的视角，而且以通俗、有趣的语言极大地增强了可读性，彰显了金华地区馆藏文物的精髓所在。

《婺宝传奇》即将出版，这是馆校合作的又一次高潮。诚然，它的出版与金华市博物馆、上海财经大学浙江学院编辑团队的努力协作是分不开的，双方旨在进一步宣传金华地区深厚的文化底蕴，让更多的人了解金华丰富的物质遗存、悠久的历史文化，以此实现更加广泛的传播。

编　者

2023年1月

【目录】

第一部分　金华市博物馆馆藏精品鉴赏　Collections of the Jinhua Museum

　　第一章　陶风瓷韵——陶瓷器　The Charm of Porcelains / 2

　　第二章　吉金耀采——青铜器　The Wonders of Bronze Ware / 48

　　第三章　金辉玉蕴——金银玉器　The Delicacy of Gold, Silver and Jade Ware / 72

　　第四章　翰墨文心——书画　Ingenious Paintings and Calligraphy / 84

第二部分　金华各县市博物馆馆藏精品图鉴　Collections of Jinhua Museums

　　第五章　兰溪市博物馆　Lanxi Museum / 106

　　第六章　义乌市博物馆　Yiwu Museum / 128

　　第七章　东阳市博物馆　Dongyang Museum / 157

　　第八章　永康市博物馆　Yongkang Museum / 181

　　第九章　武义县博物馆　Wuyi Museum / 196

　　第十章　浦江博物馆　Pujiang Museum / 213

　　第十一章　磐安县文物管理办公室　Office of Artifact Management of Pan'an County / 228

第三部分　难字阐析　Interpretation of Difficult Words

　　第十二章　八婺古韵——金华市博物馆历史文化陈列展览难字解读
　　The Ancient Bawu: Interpretation of Difficult Words Displayed in the

Historical and Cultural Exhibition of Jinhua Museum / 240

第十三章　神奇大地——金华地质文化陈列展览难字解读

Land of Wonders: Interpretation of Difficult Words Displayed in Jinhua Geological Cultural Exhibition / 252

第十四章　乡土民风——金华文化遗产陈列展览难字解读

Folk Customs: Interpretation of Difficult Words Displayed in Jinhua Cultural Heritage Exhibition / 255

第十五章　百工之乡——金华工商文化陈列展览难字解读

Land of Handicrafts: Interpretation of Difficult Words Displayed in Jinhua Industrial and Commercial Cultural Exhibition / 257

第一部分 金华市博物馆馆藏精品鉴赏

Part 1
Collections of the Jinhua Museum

第一章 陶风瓷韵——陶瓷器
The Charm of Porcelains

古陶瓷，是我国古代最具代表性的历史遗存之一。史前一万年上山文化遗址出土的陶质敞口盆、陶杯等陶器让我们看到了当时人们生活中常用的祭祀、饮食器具。商周至两汉时期的原始瓷让我们感受到中原地区礼制的正统与威严。新石器时代晚期开始出现并一直延续至汉代的印纹硬陶是由陶到瓷的过渡。成熟于东汉中晚期的婺州窑青瓷在胎土用料、上釉工艺和装烧方式等方面都有别于前期的陶器、原始瓷和印纹硬陶，可以被看作一个相对独立、系统的瓷窑体系。因此，相关研究就显得尤为必要。

Ancient porcelain is one of the most representative historical relics of ancient China. Pottery open pots, cups and other pottery wares unearthed at the site of the Shangshan Culture 10,000 years ago show us the rituals and eating utensils commonly used in people's daily life at that time. Primitive porcelain from the Shang, Zhou to the Han Dynasty presents us with the orthodoxy and majesty of the ritual system from the Central Plains, while hard pottery with printed marks that emerged in the late Neolithic period and existed in the Han Dynasty fills the transition from pottery to porcelain. Celadon of Wuzhou kiln, which fully developed in the middle and late Eastern Han Dynasty, is different from the pottery, primitive porcelain and hard pottery with printed marks in terms of material, glazing and firing, and can be regarded as a relatively independent, systematic system of kilns. Therefore, the study of it is particularly necessary.

婺州窑，因唐时窑场所在地为婺州而得名，主要分布在浙江省中西部地区的金衢盆地和江西玉山一带。它于东汉中晚期创烧出了釉面玻化度高、胎质细腻的成熟青瓷，并在六朝得以发展。唐早期除烧造青瓷外，人们还开始烧造乳浊釉瓷，在晚唐、五代、北宋早期达到鼎盛，元以后衰败。汉时已出现堆塑，化妆土、点褐彩等工艺在西晋时期开始萌芽。入唐以后的乳浊釉瓷，更是整个江南地区众多窑场所罕见。陆羽《茶经》曰："碗，越州上，鼎州次，婺州次……"他客观地评价了唐代婺州古瓷碗仅次于越窑、耀州窑的同类茶碗，在全国窑场中位列第三。《中国陶瓷史》中提道："婺州窑在唐以前仅次于越窑。"从产品的特征看，婺州窑的风格受越窑的影响较大，两者间存在着一些共性。但由于地域上的差异，两者在胎、釉、纹饰等方面不同。宋室南渡，北人南迁带来了大量的劳动力及技术，政治中心的南移促使婺州大地制瓷业进一步发展。诸如青釉、黑釉、乳浊釉、青白釉、彩绘等产品在婺州大地百花齐放、争奇斗艳。此时的婺州窑虽已进入发展末期，但它对于当时南北地区窑业的交流、海外贸易的繁荣，乃至现如今学术研究的思考，仍然具有不可或缺的作用。

Wuzhou kiln was named after Wuzhou, the place where the kiln was located during the Tang Dynasty. It is mainly concentrated in the Jinqu Basin in the middle and western part of Zhejiang Province and around Yushan in Jiangxi Province. It created mature celadon with high degree of glaze vitrification and fine texture in the middle and late Eastern Han Dynasty, and developed in the Six Dynasties. In the early Tang Dynasty, in addition to celadon, porcelain with opacified glaze also began to be made, which reached its peak from the late Tang Dynasty, the Five Dynasties to the early Northern Song Dynasty, and declined after the Yuan Dynasty. In the Han Dynasty, there were already the craft of modeling, and techniques such as engobe coating and brown splashes began to sprout in the Western Jin Dynasty.

After the Tang Dynasty, the porcelain with opacified glaze was rare in the kilns throughout the Jiangnan region. According to Lu Yu's ranking in the *Book of Tea*, "As for bowls, Yuezhou porcelain is the best, Dingzhou porcelain comes the second, and Wuzhou porcelain ranks the third...", which objectively evaluated the ancient porcelain tea ware of Wuzhou in the Tang Dynasty as the third among the kilns throughout the country, only second to the similar porcelain wares of Yue kiln and Yaozhou kiln. *History of Chinese Ceramics* wrote that, "Wuzhou kilns were second only to Yue kilns before the Tang Dynasty." From the characteristics of the product, the style of Wuzhou kiln was greatly influenced by Yue kiln, and there were some common features between the two. However, due to regional differences, there were differences between the two in terms of porcelain body, glaze and decoration. The Song Dynasty and the people from the north moving to the south brought a lot labor force and technology, and the south shift of political center prompted the further development of porcelain making industry in Wuzhou. Products such as celadon, porcelain with black glaze, opacified glaze, greenish-white glaze, painted glaze and other products prevailed in Wuzhou and competed with each other. Although Wuzhou kiln was already in its final stage, it still played an indispensable role in the communication of kiln industry between the north and south, in the prosperity of overseas trade, and even in the consideration of academic research nowadays.

1. 商印纹硬陶罐

Pottery pot with printed marks, the Shang Dynasty

该陶罐高10厘米，口径5.5厘米，腹径10.8厘米，底径5.3厘米。敞口，圆唇，束颈，鼓腹，平底。通体拍印斜方格纹。胎质坚硬细腻，呈灰色。

The pot is 10 cm in height, 5.5 cm in diameter at the top rim, 10.8 cm in diameter at the middle rim and 5.3 cm in diameter at the bottom rim. It has an open mouth and a rim with round fringe connected to a narrowing neck, a bulging belly and a flat bottom. The whole body is printed with diagonal checkerboard streak, with hard, delicate ware and grey glaze.

印纹硬陶，简称"硬陶"。浙江地区的印纹陶至少在距今8 000年的跨湖桥文化中已经出现，新石器时代晚期印纹硬陶已经成熟，夏代晚期至商代已比较普遍，西周以后逐渐成为主流。学界认为，太湖地区是印纹硬陶的起源地。硬陶采用泥条盘筑法成型，它的胎质比一般的软陶细腻，烧造温度也更高。器表多拍印叶脉纹、云雷纹、方格纹、回纹、曲折纹、菱形纹等几何纹饰。一些带有耳的器形是手捏成形后粘贴的，通常会在器物的内壁留下指痕。硬陶虽比前期的软陶坚硬，但质地依旧粗糙，又没有釉子，大多用于贮藏的器皿。这与同时期的原始瓷在品种和功用上有着明显的区别。

Pottery pot with printed marks, or "hard pottery" for short, had emerged at least 8,000 years ago in the Kuahuqiao Culture in Zhejiang, was fully developed in the late Neolithic period, prevailed in the late Xia Dynasty to the Shang Dynasty, and gradually became the mainstream after the Western Zhou Dynasty. Scholars believe that the Taihu area is the origin of pottery pots with printed marks. The hard pottery was created with the method of clay strip construction, whose texture would be finer than that of ordinary soft pottery, and firing temperature required would also be higher. The surface of the pottery was often stamped with geometric patterns such as veins, cloud and thunder patterns, checkerboard patterns, retraction patterns, zigzag patterns, and lozenge patterns. Some forms of wares with handles were shaped and pasted by hand, therefore, there would be fingerprints on the interior of the wares. Though hard pottery was harder than the previous soft pottery, the texture of it was still rough and unglazed, and was usually used for storage, which was significantly different from the primitive porcelain of the same period in terms of variety and function.

2. 汉釉陶熏炉
Pottery glazed censer, the Han Dynasty

该熏炉通高15.5厘米，口径8.2厘米，腹径17.5厘米，底径16厘米。器形扁圆，呈"炉"形。器身敛口，溜肩，腹微鼓，平底，底部附三蹄形小足。肩两侧置对称竖系，双系间饰两道浅凹弦纹。上置一盖，盖面镂两小圆孔，盖顶附钮，钮饰为鹤首。通体施褐色釉，褐中泛黄，釉面饱满润泽。胎质细腻，呈褚红色。胎、釉结合较好。

The censer is 15.5 cm in height, 8.2 cm in diameter at the top rim, 17.5 cm in diameter at the middle rim and 16 cm in diameter at the bottom rim. The object takes on the oblate spheroid shape of a "burner", which converges on the top and slants on the shoulder. It has a slightly bulging belly and a flat base with three hoof-shaped legs, together with two vertical loops on both shoulders symmetrically and two shallow bowstring patterns in between. On top of the ware is a cap that has the decoration of two small round holes cut off from the surface and a crane-head-like knob on the top. The brown-yellow glazed surface covers the ochre ware, manifesting a smooth and delicate combination of the two.

汉朝建立初期，由于饱受战祸之苦，百废待兴，统治者推崇道家思想作为治国思想以求得休养生息。自先秦时期以来的道家思潮得以巩固和完善。道家信奉大道无为、永恒不灭，认为人可以经过修行而达到神仙境界，可升天而长生不死。汉朝的器物装饰上都带有道家的元素，鹤就是典型的纹样之一。作为当时人们对于神仙的一种思想崇拜，道家视鹤为仙的化身，一鸟之下，万鸟之上，代表着长寿，是延年益寿的象征之物。西汉《列仙传》中便有仙人王子乔乘白鹤的故事记载。《相鹤经》记载："盖羽族之宗长，仙人之骐骥也。"鹤与仙人相伴，且是仙人的坐骑，"驾鹤西去"由此而来，这在一些贵族墓葬壁画中尤为明显。在熏炉内燃上熏香，合上盖，香气通过出烟孔缓缓溢出，弥漫着的香气缠绕着展翅欲飞的仙鹤，犹如一幅驾鹤升天的美景。这就是世人眼中的仙界。

In the early days of the Han dynasty, as the dynasty was plagued by wars, the society was in a state of ruin, whereas the rulers advocated Taoism as a philosophy of governance in order to recuperate. The Taoist ideologies since the Pre-Qin period had been consolidated and perfected. The Taoists believed in the inaction and immortality of the Great Dao, and believed that one could reach the realm of immortality through cultivation, and could ascend to heaven and alive forever. In the Han Dynasty, the decorations and objects were all decorated with elements from Taoism, of which the crane was one of the most presentative motifs. As a reflection of the worship of immortals at that time, Taoist regarded the crane as the embodiment of immortality, which was only second to phoenix and above all others, representing the promotion of longevity. The story of the immortal Wang Ziqiao riding a white crane was recorded in *Legend of the Immortals* of the Western Han Dynasty. *The Book of Judging Cranes* recorded that, "The crane is the patriarch of the birds, and the mount of the immortals." The crane was accompanied by the immortals and was the mount of the immortals, from which the phrase of "the crane was driven west" was created, which was particularly evident in some of the noble burial murals. The incense was burnt in the censer and the lid was closed, and the aroma of the incense slowly overflowed through the smoke holes, and the fragrance of the smoke wrapped around the cranes that were about to fly, like a beautiful scene of a crane ascending to heaven. This was what the people saw as the world of immortals.

3. 西汉原始瓷鼎
Primitive porcelain tripod, the Western Han Dynasty

该鼎高18厘米，腹径13厘米，底径9.3厘米。子母口，深弧腹，平底，下承三足。口沿两侧贴塑对称长方形耳，耳中部镂空，上端外撇。鼎盖呈覆钵形，盖面均匀堆塑三个锥形纽。器盖顶部施青黄色釉，灰褐色胎。

The tripod is 18 cm in height, 13 cm in diameter of the middle rim, and 9.3 cm in diameter of the bottom rim. It has a paired mouth, with a deep arched belly and a three-legged flat bottom. Symmetrical rectangular handles are modeled on both sides of the mouth rim, with the middle of which hollowed out, and the upper end flared out. The lid of the tripod takes the shape of an overturned bowl, with three conical buttons uniformly piled on top of it. The top of the lid is covered with greenish-yellow glaze, with grayish-brown ware.

原始瓷是原始瓷器的简称。它用瓷土作胎，表面施石灰釉，烧造温度达1 200摄氏度。它可以被看作成熟青瓷早期的发展阶段，更多的是一个时代概念。它在夏末商初开始出现，至秦汉时期仍有烧造。原始瓷的发展有三个历史高峰期，分别是西周早期、西周晚期至春秋早期、战国早期。商代以豆为主，晚期还出现了罐、钵、樽等器形。西周早期以豆、尊为主，豆盘变化较大，豆柄变短。西周中期，原始瓷相对衰落。西周晚期至春秋早期器类大量增加，并开始出现日用器，前期的豆变成了圈足碟。春秋中晚期器类大量减少，以日用的碗占多数以及少量罐、盘类器物。战国早期除生产日用器皿外，还大量生产礼器、乐器、兵器等，几乎涵盖了社会生活的各个方面，此时的江南地区开始大量仿造中原地区的青铜文化。入汉以来，墓葬中常见鼎、盉、瓿、壶等原始瓷，这些器形是效仿中原地区的礼制文化而产生的，它们随着时间的推移在造型上也发生了变化。原始瓷直至东汉末期被成熟青瓷取代，至此消失。

Primitive porcelain is short for primitive porcelain and ceramics. The body was made of porcelain clay, with a lime glaze on the surface, and was fired at a temperature of 1,200 degrees Celsius. It can be regarded as the early development stage of mature celadon in terms of the age. It began to appear in the late Xia Dynasty and early Shang Dynasty, and was still made in the Qin and Han Dynasty. The development of primitive porcelain had three peaks in history, namely, the early Western Zhou Dynasty, the late Western Zhou Dynasty to the early Spring and Autumn Period, and the early Warring States Period. The ware type in the Shang Dynasty was mainly Dou (lamp), while other types such as Guan (jar), Bo (bowl), Zun (a wine goblet) emerged. In the early Western Zhou Dynasty, the wares mainly took the shape of Dou or Zun, and the plate of Dou changed greatly, while the stalk of Dou gradually shortened through time. Porcelain wares relatively declined in the middle of the Western Zhou Dynasty, while in the late Western Zhou Dynasty to early Spring and Autumn Period, a large number of ware types began to emerge, and daily-use artifacts also appeared, of which the previous Dou evolved into plates with ring foot. In the middle and late Spring and Autumn Period, the number of daily-use artifacts decreased greatly, with bowls, jars and plates accounting for the majority of the total number of utensils. In addition to the production of daily utensils, a large number of ceremonial vessels, musical instruments, weapons, etc. were produced in the early Warring States Period, covering almost every aspect of social life. At this time, the Jiangnan region began to imitate the bronze civilization of the Central Plains in large quantities. Since the beginning of the Han Dynasty, primitive porcelain such as Ding (tripod), He (an ancient goblet), Pou (an ancient pot), and Hu (jug) were common in tombs, and these vessels were modeled after the ritual culture of the Central Plains, which had also changed in terms of shape over time. Primitive porcelain disappeared until the end of the Eastern Han Dynasty, when it was replaced by developed celadon.

4. 东汉青瓷堆塑动物纹五管瓶
Celadon five-tube bottle with modeled images of animals, the Eastern Han Dynasty

该瓶高31.8厘米，口径6厘米，最大腹径21厘米，底径14.5厘米。瓶呈葫芦形，分为两层堆塑。上层肩部对称排列四个小罐，四小罐间贴塑四只飞鸟。主瓶口部翻沿微敛，短颈鼓腹。下层腹部贴塑三只站立状的熊，熊与熊之间贴塑蛇、猪、狗等禽兽。通体施青黄色釉不及底，胎色灰。

The bottle is 31.8 cm in height, 6 cm in diameter at the top rim, 21 cm in diameter at the middle rim and 14.5 cm in diameter at the bottom rim. The bottle takes the shape of the calabash, divided into two layers with four small jars symmetrically placed on the shoulder of the top layer, and four miniatures of flying birds in between. The main rim of the bottle with folded fringe slightly converges on the top, connected with a short neck and a bulging belly. The lower layer of the belly is decorated with three standing bears, in between of which are miniatures of animals such as snakes, pigs and dogs. The bottle is made with grey wares, and the whole body except the bottom part is covered in greenish-yellow glaze.

五管瓶，东汉、三国时期江南地区墓葬出土较为多见，来源于古代农耕社会的五谷文化，属于明器。五管瓶的产生不是一蹴而就的，存在一段演变过程。早期的五管瓶因其器身低矮浑圆也可称为"五联罐"，腹部对称贴塑四个小罐，底部通常带有三足或平底，纹饰以弦纹为主。后来器身逐渐加高呈瓶状，在瓶身肩部均匀堆塑五个罐体，并堆塑少量的人物纹和熊、蛇、猪、狗等禽兽纹。三国时期，五管瓶的中间罐口逐渐增大，周围四个小罐逐渐缩小，肩部堆塑的人物纹、禽兽纹不断增多。

The five-tube bottle, often found in the tombs of the Eastern Han Dynasty and the Three Kingdoms Period in Jiangnan area, comes from the five-grain culture of the ancient farming society, and belongs to the category of funerary objects. The creation of the five-tube bottle was not an overnight success, and there was a process of evolution. Early five-tube bottles could also be referred to as "Wu Lian Guan" due to their short, rounded bodies, with symmetrically molded four small jars on the belly and a three-legged or flat bottom, decorated with string pattern. Later, the body of the bottle gradually developed into a vase-shaped form, with five jars evenly piled up on the shoulders, with a small amount of human figures, bears, snakes, pigs, dogs or other animal figures. During the Three Kingdoms Period, the central tube of the five-tube bottle gradually increased in size, and the tubes around began to shrink with an increasing number of molded decorations of human figures and animals figures.

东汉末年，皇室昏庸。"白骨露于野，千里无鸡鸣"是当时社会的真实写照。连年的战争加上土地的荒芜，致使人口大量消亡。人们渴望安定，向往着和平。我们发现这一时期出土的五管瓶上大多堆塑着熊和蛇的纹样。熊纹饰的出现，与当时人们对熊的认识有着密切的关系。当时的人们对于熊主要有两个方面的认识。一是认为它是刚猛的象征，将它用来形容勇猛的将士。《诗》曰："维熊维罴，男子之祥。"熊罴，阳物也，强力壮毅，故为男子之祥。二是认为它是吉祥、正义的象征。人们有"伏熊枕宜男"的说法，即孕妇在睡梦中梦见熊罴之类是生男孩的预兆。蛇，在远古时期被奉为生殖崇拜的图腾，专指女性，意喻女性繁衍昌盛。《诗》曰："大人占之：维熊维罴，男子之祥；维虺维蛇，女子之祥。"人们在睡梦中梦见熊或罴都是吉祥的，生个男孩多强壮。梦见蛇也是一样的，生个女孩也漂亮。诚然，这些纹饰的出现与当时社会有紧密的关系，象征着墓主人对于繁衍后代的迫切，反映当时的人们希望家族兴旺、子孙万代的美好愿望。

At the end of the Eastern Han Dynasty, the imperial family was fatuous, and "Bones are exposed in the wilderness, and there was no chicken crowing for miles" was a realistic depiction of the society at that time. Years of war, coupled with the desolation of the land, led to the mass extinction of the population, and people longed for stability and peace. We found that, most of the five-tube bottles from this period have motifs of bears and snakes on the surface. The presence of bear motifs is closely related to the knowledge of bears at that time. People had two main aspects of knowledge about bears. First, bears were regarded as the embodiment of strength, and were used to compare to gallant soldiers, as written in *the Book of Songs*, "Brown bears are the blessing for men", for the reason that bears are strong animals. Second, bears were related to blessing and justice, with the saying that "Pregnant women dreaming of a bear is the sign of having a boy". Snakes, also, was worshiped as the totem of fertility for women in ancient times. *The Book of Songs* wrote that, in divination of ancient times, dreaming of a bear was the good omen of having a strong boy, and dreaming of a snake was the sign of having a beautiful girl. Admittedly, the appearance of these emblems was closely related to the society at that time, symbolizing the urgency of the tomb master for reproduction and reflecting the good wish of the people at that time for the prosperity of the family and the descendants.

5. 西晋青瓷谷仓

Celadon covered jar, the Western Jin Dynasty

该器通高49.2厘米，腹径25.8厘米，底径13.6厘米。器身呈橄榄形。直口微敛，弧腹，平底。上置一楼阁形盖，肩部至顶部分为三层堆塑。上层堆塑重檐楼阁，中层四角分别堆塑四个仓楼，其内与楼相通，仓楼之间有侍俑。下层堆塑门楼、方阙和护仓俑，腹部贴塑铺首衔环人物。通体施青黄色釉不及底，有剥釉现象，胎色青灰。

The jar is 49.2 cm in height, 25.8 cm in diameter at the middle rim and 13.6 cm in diameter at the bottom rim. It takes the shape of an olive, with a slightly converging fringe connected to a short, straight neck, and downward is a bulging belly and a flat bottom. On top of the jar is a pavilion-shaped cap, beneath which is a modeled sculpture dividing the part from the shoulder to the top into three layers. The first layer is decorated with eaves and pavilions, below which stand four warehouses connected to the pavilions from inside, and miniatures of guardians in between, and the bottom layer holds archways, turrets and guardians. The belly is decorated with human-face patterns with rings on it. The whole body of the jar, except the bottom part, is covered with greenish-yellow glaze, slightly peeling off from the gray ware tinted with green.

此器形又称为"谷仓罐"，属于魂瓶的一种类型。它起源于古代农耕社会的五谷文化，由东汉、三国时期的五联罐、五管瓶演变而来。这件器物的五个管口被亭台楼阁和各种堆塑所取代，肩部以上堆塑亭台楼阁、仓房和阙楼还有一些双膝跪地的奴仆，楼阁屋面常作庑殿顶并层层相叠，墙院相围回廊环绕，阙楼也是成双的，展示了墓主人生前显赫的身份和地位。肩部堆塑的盘坐佛像及腹部贴塑的青龙、白虎、朱雀、玄武，说明此时佛教、道教两家已经共生。它让我们感受到了秦汉之后，西晋新的政治、经济基础正在形成。

This type of ware is also known as "grain warehouse jar", which is also a type of funerary objects. It originated from the culture of five grains in ancient farming societies, and evolved from the five-tube bottle and Wu Lian Guan of the Eastern Han Dynasty and the Three Kingdoms Period. The five tubes of this ware was replaced by molded pavilions and other figures, with molded pavilions, warehouses, Que towers and figures of servants kneeling on their knees piled on the shoulder of the bottle, of which the roofs were often stacked on top of each other, the walls and courtyards were surrounded by corridors, and the quarries were also in pairs. It showed the prominent status and position of the tomb master before his death. The molded seated Buddha statues piled on the shoulders and the Azure Dragon, White Tiger, Vermilion Bird and Black Tortoise on the belly show that Buddhism and Taoism were already coexisting at this time, which made us feel that after the Qin and Han Dynasties, a new political and economic foundation of Western Jin was being formed.

6. 西晋婺州窑青瓷熏炉
Celadon censer of Wuzhou kiln, the Western Jin Dynasty

该熏炉高11厘米，口径10.4厘米，腹径18厘米，底径9.8厘米。短直口，圆唇、丰肩，鼓腹斜收，高圈足。口沿以下饰若干道细线弦纹，肩部置一对称绳纹横系，肩、腹部镂三排圆形孔，孔大小不一。通体施青黄色釉不及底，釉层均匀滋润。胎质坚硬，呈青灰色，胎、釉结合紧密。

It is 11 cm in height, 10.4 cm in diameter at the top rim, 18 cm in diameter at belly and 9.8 cm in diameter at bottom rim. It has a short straight mouth, round lip, full shoulders, bulging belly, and highly circled feet. Below the mouth rim, it is decorated with a number of thin string patterns, and a symmetrical rope pattern is placed on the shoulder. There are three rows of circular holes on the shoulder and belly. The holes are of different sizes. It is designed with greenish yellow glaze at the entire body, but with no glaze at the bottom. It is evenly glazed, smooth and rich. The fetus is hard and blue-gray, being completely designed with glaze.

熏炉也称"香熏"或"香炉"，是中国古代用来熏香和取暖的器物。新石器时代已出现陶质熏炉，至迟在战国时期青铜熏炉、原始瓷熏炉大量出现。由于受到等级制度的影响，熏炉当时只存在于上层社会的生活之中，属于高贵之物。

Incense burner, also called "censer" or "burner", was used for burning incense or heating in ancient China. During the Neolithic Period, pottery censers had already appeared, and bronze censers and primitive porcelain censers appeared in large quantities at the latest during the Warring States Period. Due to the influence of the hierarchy system, the censers only existed in the life of the upper class at that time and belonged to the noble things.

东汉中晚期，随着成熟青瓷的创烧，江南地区青瓷熏炉大量生产。目前，婺州地区生产的青瓷熏炉以三国时期的墓葬出土为最早。三国时，熏炉呈罐形或盆形，敛口，扁圆腹，腹较浅，平底微内凹或三矮足。口部多见对称置耳，腹部通常镂两排小圆孔。西晋时期为罐形，敛口，圆唇，短颈，扁圆腹，平底。肩部置对称双耳，炉身腹部镂三层圆形孔。从出土的资料看，魏晋以来，熏香文化深入士族阶层，熏衣剃面、傅粉施朱成为士人日常生活的一种常态。现在的南京及周边地区是魏晋时期的政治、经济中心，士族广居于此，士族推动了当时青瓷的发展，各式制作精良的瓷质熏炉在该地出土，可见一斑。而此时的婺州地区在地域上过于偏僻，经济发展及文化传播较慢，但从出土的熏炉情况看，熏香文化在婺州先民中已有传播。后期，熏炉极具观赏性，慢慢地蜕变为人们手中的把玩之物，被供奉在书桌上，与书斋结合。宋人崇尚清幽淡雅的风格，当时的文人墨客对熏香推崇有加。人们认为琴棋书画之间用熏炉焚上一炷香能使人心情平静舒畅，认为它是陶冶性情、启迪才思之妙物，成为雅文化的一种象征。熏炉成为古代宫廷和贵族，乃至市井百姓生活的重要组成部分。由此，熏炉完成了由高贵向世俗的转变。

In the middle and late period of the Eastern Han Dynasty, with the creation of mature celadon, celadon censers were produced in large quantities in Jiangnan area. At present, the celadon censer produced in Wuzhou area was unearthed earliest in the burial of the Three Kingdoms Period. During the Three Kingdoms Period, the incense burner was pot-shaped or basin-shaped, with a convergent mouth, a flat, rounded and shallow belly, and a flat, slightly concave foot or three dwarf feet. Symmetrical handles were often found at the mouth, and the belly was usually skeletonized with two rows of small round holes. During the Western Jin Dynasty, the incense burner was pot-shaped, with a converging mouth, a rounded rim, a short neck, a flat, rounded belly, and a flat base. Symmetrical handles were placed on the shoulders, and three round holes were skeletonized on the belly. From the unearthed data, since the Wei and Jin Dynasties, the culture of burning incense had been widely penetrated into the scholar class, and people all scented their clothes, shaved their faces and used make-up, which had become a norm in the daily life of the scholar. As the political and economic center of the Wei and Jin Dynasties, Nanjing and its surrounding areas were widely inhabited by scholarly families, who drove the development of celadon at that time. As a result, various kinds of porcelain censers were unearthed in this area. At this time, Wuzhou was too remote in terms of region, and the economic and cultural spread was slow, but from the censers unearthed, it also showed that the culture of burning incense had been spread among the ancestors in Wuzhou. In the later period, the incense burner became very ornamental, slowly developed into a plaything in people's hands, and was enshrined on the desk, in combination with the study. The Song people, in particular, advocated quietness and elegancy, and the literati and scholars at that time greatly admired burning incense. People believed that when it came to *qin*, *qi*, *shu*, *hua*, a column of incense burned in a censer could make people feel calm and relaxed, and it was considered to be the cultivation of temperament, enlightenment of the mind of the wonderful things, and become a symbol of elegancy. Burning incense then became an important part of the lives of the imperial family and nobility, and even the city folks. Thus, the censers completed their transformation from nobility to secularity.

7. 西晋青瓷水井、水桶

Celadon well and bucket, the Western Jin Dynasty

该水井（右）高18厘米，口径11.2厘米，底径12.3厘米。侈口，平沿，束颈，溜肩，筒腹，平底。肩部饰粗线凸弦纹一道，并贴塑四只乳钉。通体施青黄色釉不及底，有流釉现象，胎色灰。水桶（左）腰鼓形，直口，短颈，腹微鼓，平底。肩部置对称双系。通体施青黄色釉，胎色灰。

The well (right) is 18 cm in height, 11.2 cm in diameter of the top rim and 12.3 cm in diameter of the bottom rim. The fringe of the rim opens outwards with a flat top and a narrowing neck, connected with a slanting shoulder, a straight waist and a flat bottom. The shoulder is decorated with a thick, embossing string pattern, with four nails placed symmetrically. The whole body except the bottom is covered with greenish-yellow glaze with sagging drops, and the ware is grey. The bucket (left) takes the shape of a waist drum with a short, straight neck and a bulging belly and flat bottom. The shoulder is decorated symmetrically with two loops, and the whole body is covered with greenish-yellow glaze which peels off the gray ware.

此组器物为水井、水桶，江南地区西晋墓葬出土较为多见，是一类仿造墓主人生前从事生产经营或是使用过的器具而烧造的明器。井是由最初的"陷阱"演变而来，来源于古代的汲水文化。据考证，早在新石器时代河姆渡文化遗址中就发现水井的遗迹。《韩非子》曰："耕作而食之，掘井而饮之，无求于人者。"水井作为人类社会文明的标志之一，可以供人们饮水，还可用于农业灌溉和生产活动。水井的出现改变了人类逐水而居的习惯，使人类不再受地域性的约束，有效地扩大了居住范围，为人类的迁徙提供了一定的基础。有人居住的地方必须依赖于水井，水井逐渐成为百姓居住的代名词，市井生活由此而来。汉代以后，人们认为水井通神，是能够保佑家宅平安的神灵。水井便成为"门、户、井、灶、雷"五祀之一。由于水井幽深通往地下，因此人们认为它是连接生与死的轮回通道。

This group of artifacts are water wells and buckets, which are more often found in tombs of the Western Jin Dynasty in Jiangnan area. It is a type of funerary objects that imitated the tools used by the owner of the tomb for production or business before his death. The well evolved from the original "trap" and came from the ancient culture of drawing water. According to testimony, the remains of wells had been found in the sites of the Hemudu Culture as early as the Neolithic period. *Han Fei Zi* recorded that, "Plow and eat the grains, dig the well and drink the water, and there is no need to ask other for anything." Wells, as one of the symbols of civilization in human society, could be used for drinking water, as well as for agricultural irrigation and for productive activities. The appearance of wells changed the habits of human beings living by water, so that humans were no longer bound by regional constraints, effectively expanding the living area, providing a certain basis for the migration of human beings. People had to rely on wells for a living, and wells gradually became a synonym for people's dwellings, from which city life began. After the Han Dynasty, it was believed that wells were gods that could protect the family and keep the house safe. The well became one of the five rituals of "door, household, well, stove and thunder," and since the well was deep and led underground, it was believed to be a reincarnation passage between life and death.

8. 西晋青瓷虎子
Celadon *huzi* (a tiger-shaped urinary container), the Western Jin Dynasty

该器高18.5厘米，口径5.8厘米，长24厘米。蚕茧形，斜直小口，口部外贴塑虎首，背部有提梁，提梁后部饰一小尾，左右腹间各浅刻一组鸟翅纹，腹下贴塑四兽足，做蹲状。通体施青黄色釉，釉层泛细碎开片。胎色青灰，胎、釉烧结程度较高。

The container is 18.5 cm in height, 5.8 cm in diameter at the top rim, and 24 cm in length. It takes the shape of a cocoon, and has a rim with flat fringe connected to a tilted straight tube, which is decorated with embossed tiger head on the outside. A handle at the back is connected to the tiger head, and is carved with a tail at one end of it. On both sides of the container is carved patterns of wings, beneath which is four molded animal feet sitting on the ground. The container is well covered with greenish-yellow glaze, which slightly peels off from the greenish-grey ware.

虎子起源于战国，因其口部饰成张口的虎首，背部有提梁，后贴塑一尾，下有四兽足，其形似虎而得名。古人认为虎为祥瑞之兽，在器物上装饰虎的造型纹饰可以驱灾避祸。早期多为青铜虎子，汉代出现了漆器虎子。关于虎子的功用，汉代郑玄曾言道："亵器，清器，虎子之属。"虎子在当时被人们作为溺器使用。六朝时期，青瓷虎子开始大量流行，并且在造型上存在着变化。东吴时期的虎子口部饰成虎头的造型，腹部常对称刻划鸟翅纹，并置有四兽足，呈半蹲状或蹲状。西晋流行前期的风格，装饰较前期更为繁缛。自东晋以来，口部及器身的贴塑、刻划的纹饰大多不见，多素面无纹。后期则口部逐渐上扬，腹部多为圆鼓形的球腹，底多为平底，兽足已不见。唐以后，随着人们生活习性的转变，青瓷虎子消失。

Huzi originated in the Warring States Period. It was decorated with a tiger's head with open mouth, a handle on the back, a tail pasted at one end and four animal feet at the bottom, therefore it was called *huzi* due to its tiger-like shape. Ancient people believed that the tiger was auspicious beast, and decorating the motifs of tiger on objects could ward off disaster. There were mostly bronze *huzi* in the early stage, and lacquer *huzi* appeared in the Han Dynasty. As for the function of *huzi*, Zheng Xuan of the Han Dynasty once said, "*Huzi* belongs to the category of urination ware." *Huzi* was used as a urination container at that time. During the Six Dynasty, celadon *huzi* began to prevail, and changed a little in the shape. During the Eastern Wu period, the mouth of *huzi* was decorated as a tiger head, with symmetrical carved patterns of wings on the belly and four half-squatting or squatting animal feet. In the Western Jin Dynasty, previous style was prevailing again, with more elaborate decorations than before. Since the Eastern Jin Dynasty, the molded decorations at the mouth or on the surface of the ware, and the carved patterns on the surface disappeared, and most of them were plain, with no decorations or patterns. In later period, the mouth of the ware was gradually raised, most belly became spherical and bulging, with a flat bottom, and the animal feet also disappeared. After the Tang Dynasty, as people's daily habits changes, celadon *huzi* also disappeared from people's lives.

9. 西晋青瓷狗圈
Celadon dog pound, the Western Jin Dynasty

该器高4.7厘米，口径12.7厘米，底径8厘米。圈钵形。口稍敛，圆唇，腹微鼓，平底内凹。腹外壁饰一圈网格纹，其内捏塑一狗，其造型生动活泼，呈作卧姿，前爪外伸，抬后腿用爪挠痒，头歪斜。通体施青黄色釉，釉层不均，仅外底露胎。胎色灰，胎、釉烧结程度较好。

The object is 4.7 cm in height, 12.7 cm in diameter at the top rim and 8 cm in diameter at the bottom rim, which takes the shape of a bowl with a round, slightly fringed and connected to a bulging belly and a downward-concaved bottom. The surface of the outer side is decorated with a mesh pattern, inside of which is a delicate modeled prone dog, with its front paws stretching and back paws scratching on its tilting neck. The object is well covered with rough a greenish-yellow glaze, with the grey ware exposed at the bottom.

狗圈，江南地区西晋时期墓葬出土较为多见，为明器的一种样式。狗，又名"犬"，经野狼驯化而来，是人类最早驯化的家畜之一。新石器时代遗址中发现狗的骨骼化石。《礼记》曰："小曰狗，大曰犬，卷毛有悬蹄者为犬。"狗作为古代人们饲养的家畜，早期也被用作祭祀。人们的生活同样也离不开狗，狗扮演的角色大致分为用于狩猎的田犬、看家护院的吠犬和供人食用的肉犬。魏晋时期，饲养狗的现象更为普遍，人们专门建造狗舍供饲养、观赏，并且士族阶层还常以狗互斗为娱乐。当时狗的价值很高，有"一狗值数十匹，御狗率具缨，值钱一万"的说法。

Dog pound, often seen in the excavations of the Western Jin Dynasty tombs in Jiangnan area, is a style of funerary objects. The dog, also known as "Quan", was domesticated from wolves and was one of the earliest domesticated animals. Fossilized bones of dogs were found in Neolithic sites. *The Book of Rites* wrote, "The small ones are called Gou, the large ones are called Quan, and the ones with curly hair and hanging feet are also Quan." As a domestic animal kept by ancient people, dogs were also used for rituals in early times. People's life was also inseparable from the dog, the role of the dog in people's lives could be roughly divided into field dogs for hunting, barking dogs to guard the home and meat dogs for human consumption. During the Wei and Jin Dynasties, the phenomenon of dog breeding became more popular, and people would build dog pounds for breeding or ornamentation, and the aristocracy would often participate in dog fighting for entertainment. At that time, the value of the dog was very high, and there was a saying of "A dog is worthy of dozens of horses, and the royal dog with a tassel is worthy of 10,000 qian".

10. 西晋青瓷猪圈

Celadon pig pound, the Western Jin Dynasty

猪圈高8.6厘米，口径13.7厘米，底径12.3厘米。猪圈呈圆筒形，平底微内凹。器身上下各刻划弦纹两道，以长条形镂空孔间隔表示栅栏，一侧有缺口作投食孔。圈内塑陶制平卧猪仔一只，长鼻，竖耳，睁目，背部刻划猪鬃，腹部点划猪毛，臀部贴塑一毛绒长尾。通体施青黄色釉不及底，浅灰胎。瓷猪长9.2厘米，宽6.2厘米，厚2.2厘米。

The pound is 8.6 cm in height, 13.7 cm in diameter at the top rim and 12.3 cm in diameter at the bottom rim. It takes the shape of a cylinder with a flat bottom slightly concaving upwards, and is decorated with string patterns both on the top and bottom.

Long strips of hollowed holes represent the fence, and a gap on one side is used for feeding. Inside the pound there is a modeled pottery prone pig, with a long nose, raised ears and opened eyes. The back and the belly of the pig is covered with carved patterns to simulate its hair, and a modeled hairy tail is connected to its butt. The whole body except the bottom is covered with a greenish-yellow glaze, which peels off from the grey ware due to its improper integration. The pottery pig is 9.2 cm in length, 6.2 cm in width and 2.2 cm in thickness.

猪圈，江南地区西晋时期墓葬出土较为多见，属于明器的一种样式。家猪起源于野猪，是古代农耕文化中的六畜之一。新石器时代遗址中就发现有猪骨骼的化石及一些外壁刻划着猪纹的出土陶器，还有捏塑成形的陶猪。此外，还发现有大量猪的下颚骨被用于陪葬的情况，这在当时被视为一种权力和财富的象征。古人还曾将猪头的造型融入龙的形象，学界认为玉猪龙就是从猪的形象演变而来的。汉晋时期出现了猪舍、猪圈一类带有猪纹的器物。《晋书》卷二十九曰："豕，北方畜，胡狄象。"早期的猪是北方游牧民族放养的牲畜，被视为胡、狄的象征。汉以后，特别是自魏晋起的江南地区社会相对安定，北方的战乱迫使人口大量南迁，致使江南一带的农耕经济得到了稳步发展，也促进了定居式养殖产业的繁荣。当时的人们把猪圈养在房子或者茅厕旁边，用于积肥，以此灌溉农田。陶猪的造型证明这时圈养的猪还处于野猪向家猪的过渡阶段。

Pig pound, often seen in the excavations of the Western Jin Dynasty tombs in Jiangnan area, is a style of funerary objects. The pig originated from wild boar and was one of the six animals in the ancient farming culture. Fossilized pig skeletons were found in Neolithic sites, as well as some excavated pottery with pig markings on the outside, and pinched and shaped ceramic pigs. In addition, a large number of pig jawbones were found to be used for burial, which was considered a symbol of power and wealth at the time. The ancients also incorporated the shape of a pig's head into the image of a dragon, and scholars believe that the jade pig dragon evolved from the image of a pig. During the Han and Jin Dynasties, a category of artifacts with pig motifs appeared, such as pig sheds and pig pounds. *The Book of Jin*, Volume 29, wrote that, "Boar, northern livestock, the symbol of Hu and Di." Early pigs were livestock raised by nomadic peoples in the north and were regarded as the symbols of Hu and Di. After the Han Dynasty, especially after the Wei and Jin Dynasties, Jiangnan area was relatively stable, and the war in the north forced a large number of people to move south, resulting in the steady development of the farming economy in Jiangnan area and promoting the prosperity of the sedentary farming industry. At that time, people kept pigs next to their houses or latrines to accumulate fertilizer, and the feces of pigs was used to irrigate farmland. The shape of the ceramic pig also showed that the pigs in captivity at this time were still in the stage of transition from wild boars to domestic pigs.

11. 西晋青瓷鸡舍
Celadon henhouse, the Western Jin Dynasty

该器高3.4厘米，长7.7厘米，宽6.6厘米。卷棚形鸡舍。卷面刻划瓦楞状纹，两端平直，平板基座，正面镂有两孔，两只鸡头伸出棚外。通体施青黄色釉不及底，胎色青灰。

The object is 3.4 cm in height, 7.7 cm in length and 6.6 cm in width. The curling shed is shaped like a henhouse with flat ends and the bottom, whose side is carved with corrugated patterns. Two holes are cut off from the front, with two modeled chickens poking their heads out of the shed. The whole object except the bottom is covered with a greenish-yellow glaze, and the body of it is greenish-grey.

古人对鸡向来怀有好感,其源自历史悠久的"鸡崇拜"。《山海经》曰:"有鸟焉,其状如鸡,五彩而文,名凤凰。"鸡通"吉",古人视鸡为灵禽,认为它是凤凰的化身。鸡作为六畜之一,早在新石器时期部分遗址中就发现鸡的骨骼化石,还有陶鸡、鸡形陶壶等出土,这些鸡形陶器可以被看作是古人对鸡崇拜的启蒙。《周礼》记载:"鸡人掌共鸡牲,辨其物……凡祭祀,面禳衅,共其鸡牲。"在等级森严的周朝,宫廷专设鸡人负责守夜和报时,并掌管供给鸡牲,分辨鸡的毛色。每逢祭祀、祈祷、衅庙等,鸡人负责供应所需要的鸡牲。可见,鸡在当时是一种非常珍贵的祭品。入汉之后,鸡崇拜由神秘转向世俗并逐渐人格化,人们认为鸡能驱邪纳吉并具有优秀的品行。《韩诗外传》曰:"首戴冠,文也;足搏距,武也;敌敢斗,勇也;见食相呼,仁也;守夜不失,信也。"书中将鸡誉为五德之禽。鸡舍,江南地区西晋时期墓葬出土较为多见,为当时明器流行的样式之一。鸡舍的造型折射出庄园经济下社会的局部面貌,与先秦时期"鸡栖于埘""鸡栖于树"的场景有所不同。

The ancients have always had a fondness for chickens, which originated from a long history of worship of chicken. *Classics of the Mountains and Seas* wrote that, "There is a bird, the shape of which is like a chicken, the body of which is colorful, named phoenix." The chicken is a homophone for "auspiciousness" in Chinese, and the ancient Chinese regarded chickens as spiritual birds and believed them to be the embodiment of the phoenix. As one of the six domestic animals, fossilized chicken bones had been found in some Neolithic sites, as well as pottery chickens and chicken-shaped pottery pots. These chicken-shaped pottery vessels could be regarded as the enlightenment of the ancient people's worship of chicken. *Rites of the Zhou Dynasty* wrote that, "(The priest) is in charge of the chicken and animals used for sacrifice, distinguishing the animals. In a sacrifice, the priest would pray for blessings, or do the ritual by sacrificing the chicken and animals." In the hierarchical Zhou Dynasty, there was a special chicken man who was responsible for keeping watch at night and telling the time, and also supplying chickens, distinguishing the color of chickens, and supplying the necessary chickens for sacrifices, prayers, rituals and so on. It is evident that the chicken was one of the most precious sacrifices at that time. Since the beginning of the Han Dynasty, the worship of the chicken changed from mystical to secular and gradually became personalized, and it was believed that the chicken could drive away evil spirits, bring auspiciousness, and had good characteristics. *Han Shi Wai Zhuan* wrote that, "The chicken has a crown on its head, which represents elegance; it takes big steps, which represents valiance; it dares to fight the enemies, which represents the courage; it calls each other for food, which represents benevolence; and it never fails to keep watch at night, which represents integrity." It hailed the chicken as a bird of five virtues. Henhouse, commonly seen in the excavations from the tombs of the Western Jin Dynasty in Jiangnan area, is one of the popular style of funerary objects at that time. The shape of the chicken coop reflected the local landscape of the manorial economy at that time, which was different from the pre-Qin period when "chickens perched in chicken roosts" and "chickens perched on trees".

12. 西晋青瓷兔纹插

Celadon flower holder with the design of a rabbit, the Western Jin Dynasty

该器高7.2厘米，口径2.2厘米，腹径9.9厘米，底径5厘米。直口，圆唇，扁圆腹，平底微内凹。肩部饰弦纹一圈，上腹正面贴塑一兔首，双眼微凸，两眼之上贴塑两耳。另一侧肩部则塑一短尾，腹部贴塑四肢。通体施青黄色釉不及底，釉面饱满滋润。胎色灰，胎、釉烧结程度较高。

The object is 7.2 cm in height, 2.2 cm in diameter at the top rim, 9.9 cm in diameter at the middle rim and 5 cm in diameter at the bottom rim. It has a rim with a flat, round fringe connected to an oblate spheroid belly, with a slightly downward concaving bottom. It is decorated with a string pattern on its shoulder, and a rabbit head with slightly bulging eyes and long ears is attached to the front of the body, with a short tail on the back and four paws on the sides. The whole body except the bottom is smoothly covered with a greenish-yellow glaze, which is well combined with its grey ware.

兔子是古代六兽之一，早在远古时期，它就是人类狩猎的猎物。战国时期的《竹书纪年》中首次出现关于兔子的记载。《古今注》曰："成帝建平元年，山阳得白兔，其目赤如朱。"书中描述了兔子的生动外形。兔子的形象同时也出现在早期的玉器、青铜器等器型中，多呈现跳跃飞奔的姿态。

The rabbit was one of the six beasts in ancient time, and had long been the prey hunted by human beings. The first record of rabbit was in *Zhu Shu Ji Nian* of the Warring States period. *Gu Jin Zhu* wrote that, "In the first year of Jian Ping of Emperor Cheng's reign, a white rabbit with eyes as red as vermilion was found in Shanyang." It depicted the vivid appearance of the rabbit. The image of the rabbit also appeared in early jade and bronze wares, mostly in a jumping and galloping posture.

随着青瓷的成熟创烧，带有兔子纹饰的青瓷大量出土于江南地区西晋时期的墓葬。目前发现的品种有兔形插、兔形砚滴等。汉代以前，古人认为兔子没有雄者。入唐以后，兔子与嫦娥联系在一起，人们认为兔子是阴性动物，是繁衍的象征。我们还发现装饰在青瓷上的兔纹大多呈现静坐和伏卧的形态，这与先前的兔子形态是完全不同的。

With the maturation of celadon, celadon with rabbit motifs were found in a large number of tombs of the Western Jin Dynasty in Jiangnan area. The varieties found at present are rabbit-shaped stick, rabbit-shaped inkstone and so on. Before the Han Dynasty, the rabbit was identified as female. The rabbit was deified in the eyes of the ancients and associated with Chang'e, and was believed to be a feminine animal and a symbol of reproduction from the Tang Dynasty. we could find that most of the rabbit motifs decorating celadon porcelain show a sedentary and ambulatory form, which was completely different from the earlier forms.

13. 西晋青瓷狮形器
Celadon ware with a design of a lion, the Western Jin Dynasty

该器高13.4厘米，口径3.3厘米，长17.5厘米。该器呈卧狮状，张口利齿，昂首目视前方，短竖耳，耳须刻划灵动。一扁平尾粘贴于臀部，背附一管形插口，口微敞。腰间刻划鸟翅纹，下承四兽足。通体施青黄色釉，胎色灰，胎、釉烧结程度较高。

The ware is 13.4 cm in height, 3.3 cm in diameter at the top rim and 17.5 cm in length, which takes the shape of a prone lion looking at the front, with its ears raised, decorated with vivid patterns, and its mouth opening showing its sharp teeth. A flat tail is attached to the butt of the lion, and a tube slot is placed on the back of it. The lion opens its mouth slightly. On the waist of the lion is the pattern of wings, below which are four paws at the bottom of the body. The whole body is covered with a greenish-yellow glaze, which is well combined with the grey ware.

狮子，古称"狻猊"，汉代以前国内没有狮子，它属于外来动物。据《后汉书·西域传》记载："章帝章和元年，遣使献师子、符拔。"公元87年，远在西域的安息国通过陆上丝绸之路，向汉室进贡狮子，此后西域各国陆续向中原朝廷进贡狮子，直至盛唐。早期的狮子只被饲养在皇宫内院里，代表着神圣和威严，平民是见不到的。随着佛教的进一步传入，人们认为同是来自西域的狮子是佛教的载体，狮子的神圣、威严与佛教的形象相结合。两晋时期，江南地区出现了大量仿动物形的青瓷产品，狮形插器就是其中之一。关于这类器物的功用，学界认为其背上的管状口应为插烛所用，称其为"狮形烛台"。狮形烛台的造型在两晋时期各有变化，西晋时烛台采用范制技法左右对接粘合成型，在器物的中间可见明显的一圈凸起的中轴范线痕迹，腹部两侧贴塑或刻划鸟翅纹。东晋时则采用拉胚成型法，器物中间的中轴范线消失，腹部两侧的鸟翅纹也不见了。

The lion used to be called Suan Ni in ancient China. There were no lions in China before the Han Dynasty, and the lion was an exotic animal. According to the *Book of the Later Han Dynasty — A Biography of the Western Regions*, "In the first year of Zhanghe of Emperor Zhang, an envoy sent Shi Zi and Fu Ba." In 87 AD, the Parthian Empire in the far west paid tribute of lions to the Han Dynasty through the overland Silk Road, and since then, countries in the west sent lions to the Chinese court until the Tang Dynasty. In early times, the lion was kept only in the inner courtyard of the palace, representing sacredness and majesty, and could not be seen by the general public. With the further introduction of Buddhism, it was believed that the lion, also from the West, was the carrier of Buddhism, and the sacredness and majesty of the lion was combined with the image of Buddhism. During the two Jin Dynasties, there were a large number of animal-shaped celadon products in Jiangnan area, and lion-shaped stick was one of them. As for the function of these artifacts, the scholars believe that the tubular mouth on the back should be used to fix the candles, and called it "lion-shaped candlestick". The shape of lion-shaped candlesticks varied in the two Jin Dynasties. In the Western Jin Dynasty, the modeling technique was adopted, and the object was bonded together with a trace of convex central axial line in the middle, and the two sides of the belly were molded or engraved with bird-wing patterns. In the Eastern Jin Dynasty, the method of throwing was adopted, and the central axial line disappeared, as did the bird-wing marks on both sides of the belly.

14. 西晋青瓷勺子、镦斗

Celadon spoon and Jiaodou (a household utensil with three legs at the bottom and a handle on the side), the Western Jin Dynasty

勺高4.7厘米，长10.5厘米，宽3.3厘米。勺呈水滴形，曲柄，通体施青黄色釉，胎色青灰。镳斗高6.5厘米，口径10.8厘米，底径5厘米。镳斗撇口，尖唇，弧腹，圜底，下承三足。一曲柄贴塑口沿至腹部，口沿及下腹饰弦纹数道。通体施青黄色釉，胎色青灰。

The spoon is 4.7 cm in height, 10.5 cm in length and 3.3 cm in width. The spoon takes the shape of a water drip, with a curved handle attached to it. It is covered with greenish-yellow glaze all over, much of which peels of from the bluish grey ware. The Jiaodou is 6.5 cm in height, 10.8 cm in diameter of the top rim and 5 cm in diameter of the bottom rim. The Jiaodou has a trumpet-like fringe, with a slightly bulging body which contracts to the bottom. It is supported by three feet on the bottom, and a handle is attached to the side of the belly of the object, which is decorated with several string patterns on the rim and the side. And it is made with greenish-grey ware, with greenish-yellow glaze covering it all over.

镳斗，又名"刁斗"，是一类敞口深腹、腹一侧置有长柄、下有三足的器物，流行于两汉至唐。唐代颜师古在《急就篇》中解释曰："鐎谓鐎斗，温器也。"可见，镳斗在古时是作为炊器使用的。早期镳斗多见于青铜器、漆器。魏晋时期，江南地区成熟青瓷兴起，受"事死如事生"观念的影响，在同时期的墓葬中发现大量的瓷质镳斗，这是人们为陪葬而烧造的明器。通过这件器物，我们可以看到当时镳斗的基本造型。镳斗作为一种炊器已融入人们的生活，唐代以后镳斗的造型产生了许多变化。

Jiaodou, also called diaodou, is a kind of deep container with open mouth, a long handle on one side and three feet at the bottom, and was popular from the two Han Dynasties to the Tang Dynasty. Yan Shigu of the Tang Dynasty explained in his *Ji Jiu Pian*, that "Jiao, also called Jiaodou, is a heating vessel." Therefore, Jiaodou was used as a cooking vessel in ancient times. In early times, Jiaodou was mostly bronze or lacquer. In the Wei and Jin Dynasty, mature celadon began to prevail. Influenced by the concept of treating the death as treating the life, a large number of porcelain Jiaodou was found in the tombs of the same period, which was a funerary object made for burial. From this ware, we could see the basic shape of Jiaodou at that time. Jiaodou had been integrated into people's lives as a cooking vessel, whose shape had changed over time after the Tang Dynasty.

15. 东晋青瓷褐彩鸡首壶
Celadon pot with brown splashes and a chicken-head-shaped spout, the Eastern Jin Dynasty

该壶高23.9厘米，口径8厘米，腹径19.5厘米，底径11.8厘米。浅盘口，圆唇，粗长颈，广肩，鼓腹下收，平底。肩部一侧置一鸡首流，另一侧附圆柱形执柄连接盘口与肩部，肩部另两侧置对称桥形系，并饰弦纹一道。通体施青黄色釉不及底，釉层莹润，盘口、鸡首及执柄处饰不规则褐色点彩。胎色灰，胎、釉烧结程度较高。

The pot is 23.9 cm in height, 8 cm in diameter at the top rim, 19.5 cm in diameter at the middle rim and 11.8 cm in diameter at the bottom rim. It has a short rim with round fringe, a thick and long neck, a broad shoulder and a bulging belly converges at the flat bottom. On one side of the pot it is decorated with a modeled chicken-head-shaped spout, while on the other side there is a cylinder handle attached to the top rim and the shoulder. The shoulder is decorated with two symmetrical bridge-like loops with a string pattern. A greenish-yellow glaze smoothly covers the whole body except the bottom, with brown splashes randomly scattered on the rim, the spout and the handle. The glaze is well combined with its grey ware.

鸡首壶，因壶嘴做成鸡首而得名，流行于西晋至唐早期，江南地区的墓葬出土较为多见。不同时期的鸡首壶造型、纹饰风格各异，特征明晰。

The pot with chicken-head-shaped spout got the name due to its chicken-head-shaped spout. It prevailed from the Western Jin Dynasty to early Tang Dynasty, and was commonly seen in the excavations of the tombs in Jiangnan area. The shape and style of decoration of the pot varied through time, with distinctive features.

西晋：器身较为矮扁，浅盘口，束颈，圆腹。肩部一侧贴塑一鸡首，鸡首无冠无颈，鸡喙与壶身不通，另一侧贴塑鸡尾，肩部另两侧对称置系。肩部纹饰多样，通常饰弦纹、连珠纹、斜方格网纹的组合纹样，并常见贴塑铺手衔环装饰。三国时期，鸡首壶出土较少见。观其形，鸡首相较于西晋时期的体量更大。

The Western Jin Dynasty: the body of the ware was relatively short and flat, with shallow plate, narrowing neck and a spherical belly. A chicken head was molded on the shoulder with no crown or neck, and the beak was not interiorly connected to the body of the pot. A chicken tail was molded on the other side, with two symmetrical loops on the other two sides of the shoulder. The shoulder was decorated with various patterns, usually with a combination of string, bead, and diagonal checkerboard patterns, and was often decorated with armorial rings. In the Three Kingdom Period, it was unusual to see the unearthed pot like this. In terms of the shape, the pot with chicken head is large in the Western Jin Dynasty.

东晋：器身较前期瘦高。鸡首高冠引颈，鸡喙与壶身相通。前期的鸡尾贴塑消失，演变成一圆柱形弧柄连接盘口与肩部。前期肩部的组合纹样消失，仅见弦纹装饰，肩部两侧置系多见桥形。晚期出现了龙形柄，并在盘口口沿、握柄、鸡首部位施褐色点彩，点彩较为规整。

The Eastern Jin Dynasty: the body of the ware was thinner and taller than that of previous wares. The chicken head had high crown with raised neck, whose beak was connected to the body of the pot. The previous molded chicken tail disappeared, and developed into a cylindrical, curved handle connecting the plate and the shoulder. The pattern combination on the shoulder also disappeared, with only string patterns left. And the loops on both sides of the shoulder were mainly bridge-shaped. And at the late Eastern Jin Dynasty, there were also regular brown splashed on the rim of the plate, the handle and the chicken head.

南朝：器身更加瘦长，盘口增大加深，颈部加长，腹部加深。握柄由圆柱体演变为龙形柄，柄上端饰成龙首，出现双鸡首造型。腹部多刻划莲瓣纹，点褐彩工艺较前期多而密，呈不规则布局。

The Southern Dynasty: the body of the ware was slimmer and longer, with larger, deeper spout, longer neck and deeper belly. The handle evolved from a cylinder to a dragon-shaped handle, whose upper end was decorated as dragon head, and double-chicken-head style emerged. The belly of the pot was commonly decorated with patterns of lotus petals, with more irregularly arranged brown splashes.

隋唐：器身呈橄榄形，上腹较为圆鼓，下腹瘦长，显得更加瘦高。鸡首曲颈高昂，鸡喙与壶身多不通。壶颈开始出现装饰纹样，常饰以竹节纹。

The Sui and Tang Dynasties: the ware took the shape of an olive, with a rounded upper belly and slim lower belly, which made the ware much slenderer. The ware had curved, raised neck, with a beak that was not interiorly connected to the body of the pot. The neck of the body began to be decorated with pattern, normally patterns of bamboo knots.

唐以后，国家统一、民族融合造就了社会的祥和稳定，社会的发展促使人们审美认知提升。壶上的鸡首演化成了短直流，鸡首壶逐渐被注子所替代，注子的产生也预示着一个不同于以往的全新社会的到来。

After the Tang Dynasty, the country was unified and the integration of ethnic groups created a peaceful and stable society, which encouraged the Tang people to improve their aesthetic knowledge. The chicken head on the pot evolved into short-straight tube, and the pot with chicken-head-shaped spout was replaced by Zhuzi (an ancient wine vessel), the creation of which also heralded the arrival of a whole new society different from the previous one.

16. 东晋青瓷褐彩灯
Celadon lamp with brown splashes, the Eastern Jin Dynasty

　　该器高13厘米，口径8.6厘米，底径8.4厘米。灯盏由油盏、支柱、承盘三部分组成。油盏为一敞口浅腹小碗，置于上细下粗的支柱上。承盘敛口平沿，斜直腹，平底。外底中部有一圆孔与支柱相通，盏口沿处饰有数个不规则褐色点彩，并刻划弦纹一道，支柱上部饰弦纹两道。通体施青色釉不及底，釉层均匀润泽。底部留有七个泥点垫烧痕，胎色青灰，胎、釉烧结程度较高。

　　The lamp is 13 cm in height, 8.6 cm in diameter at the top rim, and 8.4 cm in diameter at the bottom rim. The lamp is made up of a shallow bowl for holding oil, a support and a plate, with the bowl placed on the support that is thick at the bottom and thin at the top. The plate has a converged rim with flat fringe, and a tilt straight belly, which converges to the flat bottom, and a hollow hole in the middle of the bottom, which connects with the support from inside. The fringe of the rim is decorated with several brown splashes and a string pattern, and another two string patterns twine round the support. The whole object except the bottom is well covered with green glaze, which is in good combination with the greenish-grey ware, with seven burn marks on the bottom.

灯具的雏形来源于新石器时代的陶豆。早期的豆盘大而深腹，呈盆钵状，不仅作为人们的盛食器具，也用于祭祀。陶豆经过演变发展为浅盘，呈浅钵形；中柄出现并不断加高，高圈足，有的还加盖子。用来制作灯具的陶豆是一种细把浅盘，在浅盘的中央突起一个尖锥形支钉，用来支插灯芯。商周时期，青铜豆大量流行。《楚辞·招魂》用"兰膏明烛，华镫错些"来描述当时的灯具，说明战国时期灯具的铸造技术已经趋于精湛。

The prototype of lamps was pottery Dou from the Neolithic times. The plate of Dou in early stage was big and deep, which took the shape of a bowl, and was not only used as food container, but also for sacrifice. After evolution, pottery Dou developed into shallow-bowl shaped plate, with prolonged stem in the middle, high ring foot and sometimes a lid. Pottery Dou used to make lamps was a shallow plate with a thin handle, and a conical spike protruded in the middle of the plate for fixing the wick. In the Shang and Zhou Dynasties, bronze Dou was prevailing. The *Book of Songs of Chu · Zhao Hun* wrote that, "The orchid-scented candles are glorious, the gorgeous lamps are staggered," to describe the lamps at that time, which suggested that the casting of lamps during the Warring States Period had already been exquisite.

东汉中晚期，随着成熟青瓷的创烧，青瓷灯具出现。目前，婺州地区出土的青瓷灯具根据造型可分为三类，分别是烛台、油灯和灯盏。烛台是一类带有管状口，用以固定烛的瓷灯。油灯是一类由早期陶豆演变而来的由灯盘、灯柱、承盘组合而成的瓷灯。灯盏类似于敞口弧腹的小碗，内壁通常贴塑泥条以加固灯芯。造型的不同也意味着使用方式的不同。这件器物在造型上蕴含着早期陶豆的影子，印证了古代文明具有传承性且有序。

With the maturation of celadon during the middle and late Eastern Han Dynasty, celadon lamps and lanterns began to appear. At present, the celadon lamps and lanterns unearthed in Wuzhou could be divided into three types according to the shape, which were candlestick, oil lamp and lamp. The candlestick is a kind of porcelain lamp which is equipped with tubular mouth to fix the candles. The oil lamp is a porcelain lamp that evolved from early pottery Dou, and was made up of a combination of a lamp plate, a lamp post and a supporting plate. And the lamp is a small bowl with an open mouth and a curved belly, whose interior is often covered with plastic clay strips to reinforce the wick. The difference in form also means the difference in the way they were used. An object with traces of early pottery beans in its shape confirmed that ancient civilizations were inherited and in order.

17. 东晋青瓷羊水注
Celadon water dropper in the shape of a goat, the Eastern Jin Dynasty

该水注高14.5厘米，长13.9厘米，宽8.9厘米。羊昂首引颈，双目安详，两角后卷，耳竖贴角，下颌须飘，四足跪伏，细腰圆臀，腰间刻划羽翼纹，尾部平贴羊尾。通体施青黄色釉，釉面饱满滋润，胎色灰。

The water dropper is 14.5 cm in height, 13.9 cm in length and 8.9 cm in width. The goat has its head and neck raised, two peaceful eyes looking at the front, two horns curving to the back with two raised ears touching them, beard on chin hanging in the mid-air, four legs kneeling on the ground to support its thin waist and round hip. The waist of it is decorated with patterns of wings, and a tail is attached to the back of it. The object is well covered with greenish-yellow glaze all over, which is in good combination with its grey ware.

羊是我国古代最早被驯化的六畜之一。羊通"祥",由于羊的性格相对温顺,古人认为它是吉祥的象征。新石器时代的遗址中就发现有羊的骨骼化石。商、周时期的青铜器上也有它的纹样,羊与猪、牛合成"太牢",成为帝王祭祀活动中规格最高的牲畜之一。虽然社会不断进步,羊的地位却急剧下滑,人们逐渐意识到战争离不开马作为脚力,使得马的地位大幅提升。农耕技术的成熟又使得牛的重要性凸显。相比马和牛,既不能当作战时脚力又不能耕地的羊就显得不这么重要了。此后,羊仅被人们看作主要的肉食来源之一。我们发现,魏晋时期关于羊纹饰的青瓷器物造型大多为跪伏状,羊的四足是被捆绑而跪伏的,等着被人宰割而被食用。这件羊形水注就是当时比较典型的器形之一。西晋时期瓷羊的腹部鼓一些,双腹刻划鸟翅纹。东晋时期瓷羊的腹部则显得瘦小,双腹刻划的鸟翅纹也不见了。通过羊的造型,我们可以看出当时人们对生活的热爱和雅趣。另外,羊的头顶部镂一小圆孔,这个圆孔比较讲究。它有两个作用,一是作为水注的注、出水孔,二是预防瓷羊在烧造过程中炸裂而特意留下的。

Goats were one of the earliest six domesticated animals in ancient China. The goat is an interchangeable word to "auspiciousness" in Chinese, and because the goats were relatively docile, they were considered by the ancients to be a symbol of good luck. Fossilized bones of goats have been found in Neolithic sites, and on the bronze wares of the Shang and Zhou Dynasties, there were the motifs of sheep. Goats, pigs and cattle were called "Tai Lao" together, as the sacrifice of the highest standard that would be used in the sacrifice ceremony of the emperor, while later the status of goats declined sharply. The requirements of war greatly improved the status of horses, and the development of cattle farming made the cattle more important, compared of which, the goats appeared to be less significant, as they could not fight in a war, nor plow the fields. Since then, goats have been regarded as one of the main sources of meat. We found that the celadon wares with motifs of goats on it of the Wei and Jin Dynasties normally took the shape of kneeling goat, with its four feet tied, which was waiting to be slaughtered and eaten. The goat-shaped water dropper was one of the typical wares at that time. The belly of porcelain goat in the Western Jin Dynasty was more bulging, with bird-wing patterns carved on both sides of the belly, while in the Eastern Jin Dynasty, the belly of porcelain goat was relatively thin, and the bird-wing patterns also disappeared. By the shape of the sheep, we could see the passion for life and entertainment of the people at that time. In addition, there was a small round hole on the top of the sheep's head, which was very delicate. On the one hand, it was used as holes for water filling and water outlet; on the other hand, it was to prevent the porcelain goat from exploding in the process of firing.

18. 东晋青瓷三足砚
Celadon ink stone with three feet, the Eastern Jin Dynasty

该器高5.5厘米，口径16.6厘米，底径16.3厘米。直口微内敛，圆唇，折肩，斜腹，平底，下腹近底处置三足，足外撇。通体施青绿色釉，胎质较细，泛青灰色。胎、釉烧结程度较高。

The ink stone is 5.5 cm in height, 16.6 cm in diameter at the top rim and 16.3 cm in diameter at the bottom rim. The fringe of the rim is straight and converges slightly, which connects to an L-shaped shoulder, a tilt belly and a flat bottom. The object is supported by three feet, which are S-shaped and are placed near the bottom. The whole body is covered with a green glaze, which is in good combination with its smooth green ware tinted with grey.

砚，又名"砚台"，出现于汉。砚台作为文房用具的一种，主要是供研磨、调墨之用。早期的砚台大多为石质，分为圆形砚和板形砚两类。东汉时期，圆形砚在造型上发生了一些变化，砚上多了圆雕形的盖子，砚身置三只附足，这也是有足砚的起源。随着东汉中晚期成熟青瓷的兴起，瓷砚开始出现。

Yan (the inkstone), also known as Yan Tai in Chinese, emerged in the Han Dynasty. As a kind of stationery for grinding and making ink, early inkstone was mainly made of stone, which could be divided into round and plate-shaped inkstone. During the Eastern Han Dynasty, the round inkstone underwent some changes in shape, with newly added round covered lid and three attached feet on the inkstone body, which was also the origin of the inkstone with feet. With the rise of mature celadon in the mid to late Eastern Han Dynasty, porcelain inkstones began to appear.

婺州地区早期的瓷砚呈圆饼形，没有砚壁。瓷砚下承三足，三足常做成力士和熊的纹样，或贴塑兽面纹，三足低矮。西晋早期的瓷砚沿袭三国的样式，后期砚面外围一圈形成了低矮的砚壁，砚壁顶部做成子口，三足上的力士及熊形纹样不见，变成了兽面蹄足，三足也相对于前期高了一些。东晋瓷砚砚体的胎骨变厚，砚壁变高，足部仍以蹄足为主，但不见纹饰。此时三蹄足多见，还出现了四蹄足，蹄足的高度更高。纹饰仅以外壁刻划弦纹为主。南朝的瓷砚分为两类，一类延续前期的风格，但砚体趋于瘦高；另一类砚面边缘出现了较为明显的凹槽，呈渠状，凹槽较浅，凹槽开始带有蓄水的功能。子口多为敞口，底足由少增多，除传统的三足外，还出现了四足或六足，最多出现十足。底足的样式有蹄足和柱足两类，蹄足一改前期的素面风格，常以刻划的线条饰成蹄足纹样。这类带足圆盘的瓷砚也是早期壁雍砚的雏形。唐代早期圆形多足砚仍然流行，壁雍砚也较为多见。唐代的壁雍砚是在南朝的基础上变化而来的，南朝的砚壁子口多是微敞的，而唐代的则多见直口。砚面外围的凹槽南朝时浅，唐时则更深一些。两者在底足上的做法区别最大，南朝的足多见5~10个，而唐代的足更多，最多达20个。南朝时只有足，唐代则产生了足下又加圈足的样式。中唐以后，有足砚逐渐被无足砚代替。入宋以后，婺州地区北宋瓷窑出土的瓷砚样式较为单一，主要以抄手砚为主，不见圆形瓷砚。

  The early porcelain inkstone in Wuzhou was round, without inkstone wall. The bottom was attached with three short feet, which were usually made into the figures of strong men or bears, or molded with animal face patterns. The style of early porcelain inkstone in Western Jin followed the style of the Three Kingdoms, and later the outer circle of inkstone surface formed a low inkstone wall, of which the top was made into a relatively small mouth, and the patterns of strong men or bears were replaced by beast face and hoof, which were also relatively higher than before. In the Eastern Jin Dynasty, the ware of the inkstone became thicker, the inkstone wall became taller, the feet were mainly hoof-shaped, without any patterns. At this time, three hoof-shaped feet were common, and four hoof-shaped feet also appeared, with greater height. The outer surface was mainly carved with string patterns. The inkstone of the Southern Dynasties was divided into two categories, one inheriting the earlier style, but tending to be leaner and taller, and the other having more obvious, shallow canal-shaped grooves, which began to have the function of water storage. The small mouth of the inkstone was usually open, and the number of feet also increased. In addition to the traditional style with three feet, styles of four feet, six feet and even ten feet also emerged. The style of the feet could be divided into hoof-shaped feet and collar-shaped feet. Hoof-shaped feet was often decorated with hoof pattern formed by carved lines, rather than the previous plain surface. This kind of porcelain inkstone with feet is also the prototype of early Bi Yong Yan. In the early Tang Dynasty, round inkstone with multiple feet was still popular, and Bi Yong Yan was also common. Bi Yong Yan in the Tang Dynasty evolved from the style of the Southern Dynasty, of which the small mouth of the inkstone wall was slightly open outwards, while in the Tang Dynasty the design of the straight mouth was more common. The grooves on the periphery of the inkstone were shallow in the Southern Dynasty and deeper in the Tang Dynasty. The two were most different in the style of the feet, with 5~10 feet in the Southern Dynasty, and even more in the Tang Dynasty, as many as 20. In the Southern Dynasty there were only feet at the bottom, while in the Tang Dynasty there was a new style of ring foot under the supporting feet. After the mid-Tang Dynasty, inkstones with feet were gradually replaced by inkstones without feet. Since the Song Dynasty, styles of porcelain inkstones excavated from the kilns of the Northern Song Dynasty in Wuzhou area were relatively monotonous, mainly Chao Shou Yan, and round porcelain inkstones disappeared.

目前，婺州地区南宋及以后的瓷窑及墓葬未见瓷砚的出土。石砚最终回归主流，这与当时社会的进步以及人们的审美转变有关系。当然，就瓷砚而言，它的产生与演变史等同于古代文化的发展与传承史，这一发展阶段也是不容小觑的。

At present, there was no porcelain inkstones excavated from kilns or tombs of the Southern Song Dynasty and later in Wuzhou area. The stone inkstone eventually became the mainstream, which was related to the progress of society and changes in people's appreciation of the beauty. Of course, as far as porcelain inkstone is concerned, the history of its creation and evolution is equivalent to the history of the development and inheritance of ancient culture, and this stage should not be underestimated.

19. 宋婺州窑褐釉贴塑龙纹壶

Brown glazed pot with the design of a dragon, Wuzhou kiln, the Song Dynasty

该瓷壶高36.7厘米，口径10.5厘米，底径11.1厘米。浅盘口，细长颈，溜肩，椭圆腹，下腹内收，平底。颈腹部贴塑一条游龙，盘旋于云火之间。通体施褐色釉不及底，釉面泛乳浊，胎色灰。

The pot is 36.7 cm in height, 10.5 cm in diameter at the top rim and 11.1 cm in diameter at the bottom rim. It has a shallow but broad fringe at the rim on a thin and long neck, connecting to the slant shoulder and an ellipsoid belly that converges at the flat bottom. A modeled flying dragon is attached on the surface of the neck and belly, which is roaming through clouds and fire. It is made with grey ware, and the whole body except the bottom is covered with brown opacified glaze.

龙在我国是一个很古老的话题。关于龙的起源问题，学界众说纷纭，至今尚无定论。然而，龙的形象却很早就产生了。在婺州古瓷产生前的原始青瓷阶段，龙的造型已经出现。从此，龙就成为婺州古瓷中的一种重要的装饰纹样。从原始青瓷到成熟青瓷，从战国到宋元，龙的纹饰一直延续下来。在不同的历史时期，人们对龙的认识也都有一些异同。在明、清以前，人们虽然认为龙是神圣和崇高的象征，但它更多地贴近于人们的日常生活，龙的形象也由神秘而走向世俗。特别是到了宋代，在大量的堆塑瓶上出现了龙的形象，这说明作为圣物的龙的世俗化，这和明、清时期龙的皇权化是完全不同的。

The dragon is an ancient topic in China. There are many different academic opinions on the origin of dragons, and there is still no conclusive answer. However, the image of the dragon had been created very early. In the stage of primitive celadon before the creation of Wuzhou ancient porcelain, the shape of dragon also appeared. Since then, the dragon had become an important decorative pattern in ancient porcelain of Wuzhou. From primitive celadon to mature celadon, from the Warring States to the Song and Yuan Dynasties, the decoration of dragons was inherited. In different historical periods, there were some similarities and differences in people's understanding of dragons. Before the Ming and Qing Dynasties, although people's understanding of dragons was also sacred and noble, the dragon was more closely related to people's daily life, and the image of dragons also went from mysterious to mundane. Especially in the Song dynasty, the image of the dragon appeared on a large number of bottles with molded figures, which indicated the secularization of the dragon as a sacred object. This was completely different from the imperialization of dragons during the Ming and Qing Dynasties.

20. 元婺州窑乳浊釉梅瓶

Porcelain prunus vase with opacified glaze made in Wuzhou kiln, the Yuan Dynasty

左瓶通高23厘米，口径2.5厘米，腹径10厘米，底径7.5厘米。右瓶通高23.5厘米，口径2.5厘米，腹径10厘米，底径7.8厘米。敛口，短颈，丰肩，斜直腹下收，平底，上覆一杯形盖。通体施乳浊釉，有流釉现象。釉层晶莹润泽，乳浊发色月白。外底露胎，胎色深灰。

The vase on the left is 23 cm in height, 2.5 cm in diameter of the top rim, 10 cm in diameter of the middle rim and 7.5 cm in diameter of the bottom rim; while the vase on the right is 23.5 cm in height, 2.5 cm in diameter of the top rim, 10 cm in diameter of the middle rim and 7.8 cm in diameter of the bottom rim. It has a convergent mouth, connected to a short neck, a plummy shoulder, a straightly slanted belly convergent to the flat bottom, with a cup-shaped lid on the top. The whole body of the vase is covered by opacified glaze with dripping patterns. The glaze layer is crystal clear and smooth, with light-blue opacification. The dark grey ware of the outer bottom is exposed.

婺州地区早在唐代早期就开始烧造乳浊釉瓷，一直延续至宋元时期。早期的乳浊釉发色月白，晚期则以天青、天蓝色居多。其时代跨越之久、烧造品种之丰富为江南地区其他窑口所罕见。元乳浊釉瓷梅瓶就是典型的代表器形之一。梅瓶是一种贮酒器，始现于唐，流行于宋至清，直到民国时期亦有烧造。《饮流斋说瓷》曰："梅瓶口细而颈短，肩极宽博，至胫稍狭，抵于足微丰，口径之小仅与梅之瘦骨相称，故名梅瓶。"其造型一般为小口，短颈、丰肩，斜腹，平底，造型随着朝代更替不断地发生着变化。然而，梅瓶的称谓却是从明代开始的，早期的梅瓶被称为"经瓶"，这与宋代皇家的讲筵制度有关。目前，婺州地区出土的梅瓶以宋元时期居多，这组乳浊釉梅瓶的口部覆盖着一个倒扣着的杯形盖，可以从梅瓶里倒入美酒饮用。这一现象与两晋至唐婺州窑墓葬盘口壶的出土形制存在着共性，两晋至唐的盘口壶盘口上通常会倒扣一只敞口碗。这说明了婺州地区酒文化的传承。

In Wuzhou area, porcelain with opacified glaze began to be made in the early Tang Dynasty, which continued to the Song and Yuan Dynasties. The early opacified glaze was tinted with light-blue, while in the late stage the colors were normally azure or sky blue. The long history span and vast variety of it was rare in other kilns in Jiangnan area. The porcelain prunus vase with opacified glaze was one of the typical representative forms. The prunus vase is a wine container, which first emerged in the Tang Dynasty, prevailed from the Song to Qing Dynasties, and was still made till the Republic of China. *Appreciation of Porcelain in Yinliuzhai* wrote that, "The mouth or prunus vase is thin and the neck is short, with extremely broad shoulder, slightly narrow shin, and relatively wide bottom. The caliber of the mouth of prunus vase is only proportionate to the thin twig of the plum, hence it was named as prunus vase." It generally took the shape of small mouth, short neck, plummy shoulder, slant belly and flat bottom, which constantly changed with the vicissitude of the dynasties. However, the name of prunus vase started in the Ming Dynasty, and the ware was called Jingping in the early stage, which was related to the system of lecturing of the Song Dynasty. At present, most of the prunus vases excavated in Wuzhou were from the Song and Yuan Dynasties. The mouth of this prunus vase with opacified glaze is covered with an inverted cup-shaped lid on the mouth, which could be used as a cup to contain the wine from the vase. This phenomenon is in common with the shapes of Pankouhu (a pot with a plate-like spout) found in tombs in Wuzhou. From the two Jin Dynasties to the Tang Dynasty, a bowl would usually be put upside down on the plate of Pankouhu, which indicated the heritage of wine culture in Wuzhou.

第二章　吉金耀采——青铜器
The Wonders of Bronze Ware

  青铜，古称"吉金"，青铜的冶炼和铸造技术在我国发展较早，早在距今5 000多年前的马家窑文化时期，人们便开始使用青铜制品。夏、商、西周时期，青铜器作为礼乐文化的主要载体，用作"明尊卑，别上下"，彰显和维护等级制度。受中原文化的影响，金华所属的越国青铜器具有一定的中原文化特征，也形成了其鲜明的地方风格。此时期的青铜器与中原地区崇尚制作的大型礼器不同，多用作兵器与工具，表现出越国尚武的文化特征。春秋战国时期，随着礼乐制度的崩坏，青铜器失去了昔日作为礼器的崇高地位。

  Bronze was called "Jijin" in ancient times. Bronze smelting and casting technology developed very early in China. People began to use bronze products as early as the period of the Majiayao Culture more than 5,000 years ago. During the Xia, Shang, and Western Zhou Dynasties, bronze ware as the main carrier of ritual and music culture was used to "distinguish the honorable from the humble and the superior from the inferior". Affected by the culture of the Central Plains, the bronze ware of the Yue State to which Jinhua belongs not only had certain characteristics of the Central Plains Culture, but also formed a distinctive local style. The bronze wares of this period were different from the large-scale ritual vessels advocated in the Central Plains. Many of the bronzes were weapons and tools, showing the typical martial culture of the Yue State. During the Spring and Autumn Period and the Warring States Period, with the collapse of the ritual and music system, bronzes lost their former lofty status as ritual vessels.

秦汉以后，青铜器走下圣坛，多作为日常生活用具使用。熏炉、铜镜、奁等逐渐普及，成为平民可用之物。在青铜器漫长历史的不同发展阶段，社会政治制度的变革，人们思想、习俗的转变与审美艺术自身的发展，使各个时期青铜器的形制、纹饰、铭文等表现出不同的时代风貌，呈现青铜艺术之美。

After the Qin and Han dynasties, bronze wares went down to the altar and were mostly used as daily utensils. Smokers, bronze mirrors and goblet gradually became popular and available to the common people. At different stages of development in the long history of bronzes, changes in social and political systems, changes in people's thoughts and customs as well as the development of aesthetic art enabled the shapes, patterns and inscriptions of bronzes in various periods to present various styles and beauty of bronze art.

1. 商云纹铜铙

Bronze Nao with cloud patterns, the Shang Dynasty

该器口径25.9厘米，腹径28.5厘米，底径15.5厘米。铙体呈合瓦形，上窄下宽。甬上无旋且为素；钲部饰云纹和连珠纹，遂部饰饕餮纹。钲部出现四个枚，起调节音色的作用。

It is 25.9 cm in diameter at the largest rim, 28.5 cm in diameter at the middle rim and 15.5 cm in diameter at the bottom rim. The integrated-tile-shaped Nao is narrow at the top and wide at the bottom. The empty cavity without a rotary knob is plain. It is carved with cloud patterns, linked-pearl patterns and *taotie* patterns. There are four *mei*, adjusting tones.

铜铙是商代晚期流行的王室重器，是宫廷中一种地位显赫的礼仪乐器。其基本形制似铃，但有圆柱形空甬与体腔相通。使用时，铙口朝上，将空甬植于木架之上。此时的铜铙已是早期青铜钟类乐器发展成熟的产物，不仅确立了合瓦形的结构，出现了系列性的成组编铙，而且奠定了青铜乐钟"一钟二音"的基础，成为一种专用的、有固定音高、能够演奏六声甚至完整七声音阶、具备旋律性的乐器。

The bronze Nao was a popular royal instrument in the late Shang Dynasty and a prominent ritual instrument in the palace. It basically resembles a bell, but there is a cylindrical empty cavity connecting to the body cavity. When in use, the mouth is upward, and the empty cavity is placed on the wooden frame. At this time, the bronze bell had developed into a mature stage, for it not only established the structure of the integrated tiles, but also formed a serious of group Nao, preparing it to be that of "one bell and two tones". Nao hereafter becomes a dedicated musical instrument with fixed pitch and certain melody, capable of playing six tones or even full seven tones.

2. 汉铺首青铜矛
Bronze spear, the Han Dynasty

该器长28.5厘米。通体宽扁且直。前部扁平如剑为利刃，中部收缩为圆筒状，并凸饰双面人像，至后部直径增大，銎部中空便于插杆，尾部一侧有孔可系绦。

It is 28.5 cm in length. It is wide, flat and straight. The flat front part likes a sword is the sharp edge, the middle part contracted into a cylindrical shape, embossing two portraits, and the increasingly large tail part in diameter is hollow for inserting a rod. The tail part also has a hole for a silk braid to go through.

青铜矛是春秋战国时期一种常规长兵器。该青铜矛年代久远，制作工艺精湛，是金华市出土的极为珍贵的一件青铜器物。这件青铜矛的出土对研究金华及汉代社会变迁具有一定的意义。

The bronze spear was a conventional long weapon during the Spring and Autumn Period and the Warring States Period. This bronze spear is old and exquisite in craftsmanship. It is an extremely precious bronze artifact unearthed in Jinhua. This bronze spear has a certain significance for studying the social changes of Jinhua and the Han Dynasty.

3. 东汉铺首衔环弦纹铜簋
Bronze pot with animal head applique holding rings, the Eastern Han Dynasty

该器口径28.4厘米，底径16.7厘米，高14厘米。

The pot is 28.4 cm in diameter of the top rim, 16.7 cm in diameter at the bottom rim, and 14 cm in height.

簋是商周时期重要的礼器，其用途类似于现在人们吃饭用的大碗。在祭祀和宴享时，簋以偶数组合与以奇数组合的列鼎配合使用。据记载，天子用九鼎八簋，诸侯用七鼎六簋，大夫用五鼎四簋，元士用三鼎二簋。

Gui, an important ritual vessel in the Shang and Zhou Dynasties, was used as large bowls for eating. During sacrifices and feasts, the even-numbered *gui* was used in combination with odd-numbered column tripods. According to records, the emperor used nine *ding* and eight *gui*, the dukes used seven *ding* and six *gui*, the scholar officials used five *ding* and four *gui*, while *yuanshi* used three *ding* and two *gui*.

4. 东汉铺首衔环宽带纹青铜奁

Bronze goblet with animal head applique holding rings and patterns of strips, the Eastern Han Dynasty

　　该器口径21.8厘米×22厘米，高17厘米，足高3厘米。直壁，器腹较深，下有三兽足，器身被宽带纹分为上下两段，对称饰兽面铺首衔环。

　　It is 21.8 cm×22 cm in diameter at the top rim, 17 cm in overall height, and 3 cm in height of feet. It is straight and deep in belly, with three feet. This relic is divided into two sections by wide stripes, with a symmetrical pair of a beast-faced pattern and ring.

　　奁，又称樽，是战国时期出现的日常实用酒器。在汉代，酒一般被藏在瓮、榼或壶中。饮宴时，主人先将酒倒入樽中，再用勺酌入耳杯奉客。汉代的樽有盆形和筒形两大类。樽的胎骨多为铜胎或木胎，铜樽在上流社会是常见的酒器，分为有盖和无盖两种，腹部都有两个对称的铺首衔环耳，底下常有三足。此铜奁造型优美，在金华市出土的青铜器中尚属精品，对研究金华市这一时期的经济、社会风俗、手工业发展和青铜铸造工艺具有一定的意义。

Lian, also named *Zun*, a daily practical wine vessel appeared during the Warring States Period. In the Han Dynasty, wine was generally hidden in weng (jars), ke (ancient wine vessels) or hu (pots). When drinking, the wine was first poured into *zun*, and then poured into the ear cup with a spoon. There are two types of *zun* in the Han Dynasty: basin-shaped and cylinder-shaped. Most of *zun* are copper or wooden. Bronze *zun* were common wine vessels in the upper class. It is divided into two types: covered and uncovered. There are two ears with rings at the middle and three legs at the bottom. This beautiful relic is exquisite among the bronze wares unearthed in Jinhua. It has certain significance for studying economy, social custom, handicraft development and bronze foundry art of Jinhua during this period.

5. 东汉半圆方枚神兽纹铜镜

Bronze mirror with patterns of semi-circle and square patterns and mythical beasts, the Eastern Han Dynasty

该铜镜直径11.8厘米，厚0.3厘米。圆形，兽首钮，草节纹圆钮座。铜镜内区作四分法布置，以四辟邪分成四组：一组是东王公，与之相对的是西王母；另一组为伯牙弹琴，与之相对的是泰一出行。八环乳分列其间，上置神侍神兽。外饰十二半圆方枚，每枚一字。外区饰画纹带一周，卷云纹一周。

　　The mirror is 11.8 cm in diameter and 0.3 cm in thickness. The mirror takes the shape of a circle decorated with a beast head shaped button and with grass shaped button base. The inner circle is divided into four parts, of which are four groups—the East King, the West Queen, Bo Ya playing *qin* and Tai Yi going out—which are separated by eight nipple-shaped rings decorated with mythical soldiers and creatures. The outer circle is decorated with 12 semicircles and 12 squares inscribed with 12 Chinese characters respectively. The outside rim is decorated with lines and rolling-cloud patterns.

　　东汉时期是社会将要发生更迭动荡的历史时期，人们的精神生活空虚，只能通过一些神话中的人物形象和生活画面来描述他们想象中的和平与美好。道教思想在社会中占据着重要的地位，道教的各路神仙诸如三皇五帝、东王公、西王母等也纷纷登场。当人类对宇宙的认识水平及生存能力尚处在极为低下的状态时，这些神灵无疑对他们产生巨大的吸引力。道教将东王公神化为扶桑大帝尊神，象征东方的太阳之神，是天下男子凡成仙得道者必须敬奉的神灵；将西王母视为女仙的领袖，三界十方女子都是她的部下。

　　During the Eastern Han Dynasty, a historical period of social change and turmoil, people were at a loss in their spiritual life. They could only describe the peace and beauty through some mythological figures and life pictures they imagined. Taoist thought occupied an important position in the Eastern Han society. Taoist gods such as the Three Emperors and Five Sovereigns, the East King, and the West Queen emerged one after another. At a time when human kept an extremely low understanding of the universe and low capacity to survive, these gods were undoubtedly a huge attraction to them. Taoism transformed the East King into the Great God Fusang, symbolizing the Eastern Sun God.

And it is the god that all men in the world must worship if they wanted to become immortals and attain Taoism. The West Queen regarded as the leader of female fairies could command the women from the Three Realms and the Ten Directions.

"伯牙鼓琴、子期听琴"的传说在战国时期已经有文献记载。汉武帝时期盛行神仙信仰与升仙不死说,此后随着"升仙热"的不断发展,汉代社会开始对传统神仙说的内容不断进行加工改造。前代传说中的圣贤人物、先朝的帝王将相、民间流传的隐逸高士等多被纳入"仙界人物"的行列,成为世人祭祀崇拜的"仙化"对象。古代神人爱好音乐,传说中的三皇五帝均与器乐有关,如神农氏削铜为琴以通神明、伏羲作琴、舜弹五弦之琴而治天下等。伯牙被认为是当时"高士神仙化"的一个典型例证。泰一最初记载于屈原的《九歌》,是春秋至战国时期百姓所信仰和祭祀的天神。汉代,人们长期以东皇泰一作为最高祭祀正神,东皇泰一是至高神。

The legend of "Bo Ya playing while Zi Qi appreciating" had been found in the literature during the Warring States Period. During the period of the Emperor Wu of the Han Dynasty, the belief in immortals prevailed. With the continuous development of the "rise of immortality" in the Han Dynasty, the traditional stories of immortals were continuously processed and rewritten. Most of the recluse masters, the emperors and ministers of pervious dynasties as well as folkloric figures were immortalized in the groups of "fairy world" and then were worshipped. Ancient gods were excelled in music, and the legendary three emperors and five emperors were all related to instrumental music. For example, Shen Nong cut copper into the *qin* so as to communicate with gods, Fu Xi made the *qin*, and Shun played the five-stringed *qin* to rule the world. Bo Ya was a typical example of a profound scholar being immortalized. Tai Yi, originally recorded in Qu Yuan's *Nine Songs*, was the god worshipped among people during the Spring and Autumn Period to the Warring States Period. During the Han Dynasty, Donghuang Tai Yi was the paramount god.

6. 东汉青盖铭龙虎纹铜镜

Copper mirror with patterns of tiger and dragon, the Eastern Han Dynasty

该铜镜直径15厘米，厚度0.9厘米。圆形，半圆钮，圆形栉齿纹钮座。铜镜内区高浮雕有二龙一虎，龙虎夹钮对峙而立。龙脑后有一对长角，身躯隆起，尾部盘旋，露出二爪，呈躬身蓄势攻击状，背有乳状突起。两龙前后排列，造型相同。虎与龙怒目相视，肢爪飞舞。龙、虎均张口、露齿、吐舌，脸颊有飞扬的胡须，并填以几何纹象征云气。外饰铭文带和栉齿纹各一周。外区饰两周锯齿纹与一周双线水波纹。

The mirror is 15 cm in diameter and 0.9 cm in thickness. It takes the shape of a circle, with a hemisphere shaped button and a circle-shaped knob with comb patterns. Two dragons and one tiger in high relief of the inner part of the bronze mirror stands opposite each other centering around the button. There are a pair of long horns behind the dragon head, the body is bulging, the tail is hovering, two claws are exposed, ready to attack. There is papillary protrusion on the back of the dragon. The two dragons are arranged one behind the other, shaped the same. The tiger and the dragons glare at each other, their limbs flying. Both the dragons and the tiger open their mouths, showing teeth and tongues, with flying beards on their cheeks and with geometric patterns for floating clouds. It is externally decorated with both inscribed belt and comb pattern respectively. The outer part of the mirror is decorated with two circles of sawtooth patterns and one circle of double-lined water ripples.

龙虎镜是东汉时期铜镜的杰出代表，也是将高浮雕的铸镜工艺发挥到极致的一个镜种，它的兴盛反映了当时社会经济，尤其是铸造业的繁荣发展。

The copper mirror with patterns of tiger and dragon is an outstanding representative of the bronze mirror in the Eastern Han Dynasty, and it is also a mirror type that maximizes the high-relief casting technique. Its prosperity reflects the prosperity and development of the social economy at that time, especially the casting industry.

7. 西晋孔子弟子铜镜
Bronze mirror with images of disciples of Confucius, the Western Jin Dynasty

该铜镜直径16厘米，厚0.4厘米。1976年，它出土于金华市古方砖瓦厂。镜圆形，素窄缘，缘边起翘，半球形钮，圆钮座。座外纹饰区为伸展的四叶，对称分布于钮座四边，每叶内饰一人，并分别题曰："弟子子贡""弟子颜渊""弟子仲由""圣人（孔子）"。细观此镜可见四人端坐叶内，双手高举。每叶间又饰双凤及松柏图案，以示圣人的高洁儒雅。纹外还有铭文一周，为"子丑寅卯辰巳午未申酉戌亥"；依次向外为栉齿纹、锯齿纹。

The mirror is 16 cm in diameter and 0.4 cm in thickness. The mirror was unearthed in 1976 in Gufang Bricks and Tiles Plant of Jinhua City. The mirror takes the shape of a circle, with a sharp edge cocking and the back decorated with a hemisphere shaped button. The patterns around the bottom are leaves symmetrically stretching to the edge, in each of which there is a figure with its name inscribed beside, as "disciple Zi Gong""disciple Yan Yuan""disciple Zhong You" and "sage Confucius". The figures are sitting in the leaves with their hands held high, and between the leaves are decorations of two phoenixes and pine and cypress to show the elegancy and sanctity of the sages. Around the patterns of leaves are inscribed characters of the twelve terrestrial branches, and pat terns of different serrations arranged in order.

自汉武帝实行"罢黜百家，独尊儒术"的政策以来，儒家思想逐渐成为社会的统治思想。因此，汉、六朝的铜镜镜纹与铭文的一大主题便是反映汉代倡导的儒家思想及道德准则，其中，又以体现"忠"的吴王、伍子胥画像镜，以及与"孝"相关的铭文镜最为常见。这面孔子弟子铜镜，用了近似直白的题材，来体现儒家思想的重要地位，进而宣扬中国重文重教的传统。而通过孔子"农山言志"的场景，来歌颂孔子成就的器物在全国实不多见，而以此内容作为镜纹来反映当时儒家思想兴盛的器物目前仅此一件。它的出土，为研究铜镜的学者提供了珍贵的历史资料，对研究六朝时期金华地区的政治、经济、文化具有重要的历史价值。1992年，这枚铜镜被评定为"国家一级文物"。

Since the Emperor Wudi of the Han Dynasty deposed hundreds of schools and respected Confucianism only, Confucianism gradually became the ruling ideology of the society. Therefore, one of the main themes of the bronze mirror patterns and inscriptions in the Han and Six Dynasties was to depict the thoughts and moral standards advocated by Confucianism, among which the most common were the portraits of King Wu and Wu Zixu who embodied loyalty and filial piety. The bronze mirror of the disciples of Confucius could be said to demonstrate the significance of Confucianism and the tradition of emphasizing education with the most straightforward way of expression. However, few wares have been found to praise Confucius' achievements by depicting the scene of Confucius and his disciples lecturing, and the bronze mirror is the only one to reflect the prosperity of Confucianism at that time, which offered precious historical evidences for scholars to study the history of bronze mirror, and the politics, economy and culture of the Jinhua area in the Six Dynasties. The bronze mirror was designated as a national first-class cultural relic in 1992.

8. 六朝雁形铜镳斗
Wild goose copper Jiaodou, the Six Dynasties

持柄呈雁形，S型颈连盘洗，呈引颈翘首状。盘沿唇外翻一圈，尾部呈新月状，中置流口。腹部内收，圜底。三兽足，足部外撇。

The handle is in the shape of a wild goose, and the S-shaped neck connected to the plate takes the shape of a bowed head. The plate turns outwards around the rim, while the tail of the plate is crescent-shaped, and the orifice is located in the middle. It is adducted in the body, round at bottom, three-legged with feet outwards.

镦斗，又称"刁斗"。它是一种古代青铜炊具，盛行于战国、汉及魏晋时代。一般认为镦斗是一种温羹器，即军队用的一种铜制的锅，白天用它烧饭做菜，夜里做打更的柝用。此镦斗制作精良，在本地出土的青铜器物中尚为少见，故对研究金华市当时政治、军事、经济、社会生活、青铜手工业的发展具有一定的意义。

Jiaodou, also known as *diaodou*, is an ancient bronze cooking utensil. It was popular in the Warring States Period, Han, Wei and Jin Dynasties. It is generally regarded as a soup warmer, used as a copper pot by the army. It is used for cooking during the day and patrolling at night. This relic is well-made, and is rare in the bronze artifacts unearthed locally, so it has a certain significance for studying the development of politics, military, economy, social life, and bronze handicraft industry in Jinhua city at that time.

9. 唐鸳鸯麒麟纹葵形铜镜

Copper sunflower-shaped mirror with patterns of kylin, the Tang Dynasty

该铜镜直径14.3厘米，厚0.7厘米。八出葵花形，半圆钮。内区饰鸳鸯、麒麟各一对，鸳鸯对峙，上下各一麒麟。外区每瓣葵花边内饰蝴蝶、流云，相间排列。

The mirror is 14.3 cm in diameter and 0.7 cm in thickness. It takes the shape of a sunflower, with a semi-circular button. The inner area is decorated with a pair of mandarin ducks opposing each other and kylins upward and downward. In the outer area, each sunflower petal is decorated with butterflies and flowing clouds arranged alternately.

在造型方面，唐代铜镜突破了单一的圆形，出现了精巧别致的菱花形、葵花形、方形、亚字形等形式。题材方面，植物和花鸟题材增多。花鸟图案是唐代铜镜温湿度的代表纹样，也是流行时间最长、贯穿整个朝代的镜类。

In terms of shape, the bronze mirror of the Tang Dynasty broke through the single round shape, and created exquisite and unique forms such as rhombus, sunflower, square, and character of "亚". In terms of themes, plants, flowers and birds had increased. The flower and bird pattern was the representative of the temperature and humidity of the bronze mirror in the Tang Dynasty, and was also the pattern popular for the longest time through the entire dynasty.

铜镜在唐代不仅是生活用品，也被作为礼品相互馈赠。因此，具有美满幸福之意的纹样得到了人们的喜爱，这些有吉祥寓意的纹饰也代表了人们祈求平安顺遂的心理和乐观向上的审美倾向。自然界中，鸳鸯是雌雄偶居不离的。在人们心中，鸳鸯与美好的爱情息息相关，在物品上装饰这样的纹样，用以祈盼夫妻伉俪情深。铜镜中的鸳鸯也必定成双成对地出现。

Bronze mirrors were not only daily necessities in the Tang Dynasty, but also used as gifts for each other. Therefore, the patterns with the meaning of joy and happiness have been favored by people. These patterns with auspicious meaning also represent people's mentality to pray for peace and prosperity and an optimistic aesthetic tendency. In nature, mandarin ducks are couple. In people's mind, mandarin ducks were closely related to beautiful love. Such patterns were decorated on objects to pray for the love between husband and wife. The mandarin ducks in the bronze mirror were sure to appear in pairs.

10. 唐四神兽纹铭文铜镜
Bronze mirror with four mystical creatures and inscriptions, the Tang Dynasty

该铜镜直径12.3厘米，厚7厘米。圆形，饰半圆钮，连珠纹钮座。镜背鎏银，内区饰四神兽，绕钮两神兽头朝前对峙，两回顾对峙，主纹与近缘区之间饰锯齿纹两周。

The mirror is 12.3 cm in diameter and 7 cm in thickness. It takes the shape of a circle, decorated with a semi-circular button and a string-of-bead-patterned button base. The back of the mirror is gilded silver. In the inner part, there decorated with four mystical creatures, one pair of the creature heads opposing each other while the other pair turning around opposing each other. There are two circles of sawtooth patterns between the main pattern and the rim.

11. 宋婺州官铸造监铭文铜镜
Bronze mirror of Wuzhou, official ware, the Song Dynasty

　　该铜镜直径16厘米，厚0.4厘米。方形，委角，素平缘。半环形钮，镜钮左侧有一长方形方框，框内分两列竖书，楷体铭"婺州官铸造监"，后有花押。该铜镜目前确定为宋代婺州官方监制，可见在宋代婺州就设有官府铸镜机构。

　　The mirror is 16 cm in diameter and 0.4 cm in thickness. It takes the shape of a square with four corners cut off. The mirror was decorated with a half-ring-shaped button, on the left of which is a rectangle box with words written vertically "supervised by Wuzhou officials" to be followed by a sign. The bronze mirror can be determined to be produced under the official supervision of Wuzhou in the Song Dynasty, which indicates that there had been an official mirror casting institution in Wuzhou.

12. 宋湖州真石家念二叔照子心形铜镜
The heart-shaped bronze mirror with inscriptions of "Zhenshijia nian ershuzhaozi" made in Huzhou, the Song Dynasty

该铜镜纵10.3厘米，横8.3厘米。心形，素窄缘，钮残。镜背素面无纹，钮右侧长方形线框内分两列竖书，楷体铭曰："湖州真石家念二叔照子"。

The mirror is 10.3 cm in length and 8.3 cm in width. It takes a shape of heart with a sharp edge and with a broken button. There is no patterns on the back of the mirror. Along the right side of the button, there is a rectangle frame with two lines of regular scripts "Zhenshijia nian ershuzhaozi (it is regarded as the brand of the mirror) made in Huzhou".

南宋时，镜子是按重量计价的。湖州石家镜子，每两六十文，价格正好是庆元三年规定的官价收购每两三十文的一倍。此外，因宋人避讳甚严，南宋湖州镜大多称"照子"。赵匡胤的祖父名为"赵敬"，因避"镜"讳，"镜子"改为"监子"或"照子"。

Mirrors were priced by weight in the Southern Song Dynasty. For Shijia mirrors of Huzhou, it was 60 *wen* per *liang* officially, exactly double the official price of that in the third year of Qingyuan. In addition, due to the strict avoidance of taboos by the people of the Song Dynasty, Huzhou mirrors in the Southern Song Dynasty were mostly called "*zhaozi*", showing respect to the ancestor of Zhao Kuangyin (whose name had a Chinese character pronounced "jing"). In order to avoid using jing, the mirrors were named "*jianzi*" or "*zhaozi*".

13. 宋鼎式炉
Stove in shape of a tripod, the Song Dynasty

该炉口径10厘米×8.4厘米，耳高2.8厘米，炉高14.5厘米。椭圆形，立耳，折沿。耳饰草叶纹，颈部饰一周由三条弦纹组成的菱形纹，菱形纹四角内饰云纹，两云纹之间饰S型云纹，中心位置饰四雷纹组成的菱形。腹部以四道纵凸棱，将纹饰分成四区。耳下两区对峙饰雷纹。主体纹饰为前后对峙各两条螭龙，颈部交缠，回顾后望，底纹为雷纹。四兽足与腹交接处为兽面纹。

The stove is 10 cm×8.4 cm in diameter at the top rim, 2.8 cm in height of ears, 14.5 cm in overall height. It takes a shape of oval, with erect eras and folded edge. The ears of the relic are decorated with grass-blade patterns, and the neck is decorated with a diamond pattern composed of three string patterns. Inside the four corners of the diamond pattern, there are clouding patterns decorated with S-shaped clouding lines. The center part of the relic is decorated with four-thunder patterns. There are four longitudinal flanges dividing the patterns into four areas. The areas under the ears are decorated with lightning patterns. The main part of the relic is decorated with two chilong, turning round and facing each other. The bottom of the relic is decorated with thunder patterns. The beast-face patterns decorate the part connecting four legs and the body of the relic.

这是一个铜制的焚香器具。此铜器造型精美，制作工艺精湛，在当地出土铜器中尚属罕见。因此，它对研究金华市当时政治、宗教、经济、社会生活、青铜手工业的发展具有一定的意义，也从侧面反映出当地居民对祭祀礼仪的重视。

This is an incense burner made of bronze. This bronze ware is exquisite in shape and in craftsmanship, which is rare among the bronze wares unearthed locally. Therefore, it is of certain significance to study the development of politics, religion, economy, social life, and bronze handicraft industry in Jinhua city at that time. It also reflects the local residents' emphasis on sacrificial etiquette.

14. 明鎏金铜佛像
Gilded bronze Buddha statue, the Ming Dynasty

座长11.9厘米，座宽8.7厘米，底高4.5厘米，像高14.1厘米。佛高肉髻，螺发，螺发着青色，髻顶；眉间有白毫，双眼微闭，双耳垂肩；双手持法宝，左手法宝残缺；着袒右肩袈裟，下着长裤；结跏趺坐于束腰仰覆莲座上。莲台高起，上下沿各饰一周饱满的连珠纹。通体鎏金。

The overall height is 11.9 cm, overall width is 8.7 cm, and the seat is 4.5 cm in height, the figure is 14.1 cm in height. The Buddha has a topknot and small snail-shell curls on his head, which is painted bluish-green, and has white hair in between the eyebrows, with his eyes slightly closed and earlobes fall over the shoulder. Both his hands are holding the treasure, while the one held in the left hand is lost. He is wearing a cassock on the upper body and trousers on the legs with his right shoulder bared, sitting cross-legged on a high lotus seat, which is decorated with patterns of beads in a full circle. The whole statue is gilded, with some part of it rusted.

15. 明石泉春记仿汉博局纹铜镜
Bronze mirror inscribed with characters of shiquanchunji of the style of Han Bo-Ju mirrors, the Ming Dynasty

该铜镜直径10.8厘米，厚0.6厘米。圆形，圆钮，翻砂东汉早期八乳八禽规矩镜。钮座外围为双线方框，铜镜内区饰博局纹、八神纹，以及八个大的乳钉纹，外饰铭文带和栉齿纹各一周。外区饰锯齿纹、流云纹画文带。钮右侧长方形线框内竖书，楷体铭曰"石泉春记"。

The mirror is 10.8 cm in diameter and 0.6 cm in thickness. It takes a shape of a circle, with a round button, made again from the eight-nipples-and-eight-birds well-disciplined mirrors. There is a double-lined frame at the outer rim of the button. In the inner part of the mirror, there decorated with bo-ju patterns, eight-mythical-creature patterns and eight big nail patterns. The outer rim of the relic is decorated with a circle of inscription belt and a circle of comb patterns. At the outer part of the mirror, there decorated with sawtooth patterns and floating clouding belt. There inscribed with the regular characters of "shiquanchunji" inside the rectangle frame at the right of the button.

明、清时期，湖州镜再度崛起。成化《湖州府志》云："郡中工人铸镜最得法，世称湖州镜。"明代湖州镜多以东汉铜镜翻砂铸成。

During the Ming and Qing Dynasties, Huzhou mirror rose again. *The Annuals of Huzhou Prefecture* recorded that "The workers here are the best in casting mirrors named Huzhou mirrors in the world." Most of the Huzhou mirrors in the Ming Dynasty were casted from the bronze mirrors of the Eastern Han Dynasty.

16. 清薛惠公造铭文方形铜镜

Square copper mirror inscribed with "made by Xue Huigong", the Qing Dynasty

该铜镜边长7.1厘米，厚0.3厘米。方形，素宽平缘。镜背四列楷书，铭文曰："如日之精，如月之明，水开一色，犀照群伦"。其后有葫芦形"苕溪"和方形"薛惠公造"印记。

The mirror is 7.1 cm in length and 0.3 cm in thickness. It is square and plain, with flat rims. There are four lines of regular scripts at the back of the mirror, saying, "The mirror reflects as the essence of the sun and the light of the moon. It is clear as water. It reflects a real image of the object". There are also gourd-shaped *"tiaoxi"* and a square stamp of "Xue Huigong made".

明代湖州镜以薛氏所造最著名。明人刘沂春编的《乌程县志》记载："湖之薛镜驰名。薛，杭人，而业于湖。以磨镜必用湖水为佳。"湖州薛氏造镜数量最多、质地最好的是薛惠公。

The most famous Huzhou mirror is made by Xue family in the Ming Dynasty. *The Annal of Wucheng Country* recorded that "Xue mirrors are well-known. Xue, a native of Hangzhou, worked in Huzhou, using the lake water to polish the mirror for a better product." In particular, Xue Huigong made the most mirrors and the best mirrors.

17. 清铜佛像

Bronze Buddha statue, the Qing Dynasty

座高4.5厘米，像高15.2厘米，宽6.7厘米。佛高肉髻，肉髻与发饰间饰髻珠，螺发，髻顶；着袒右肩袈裟，衣纹清晰，帔帛敷搭双肩；双手于胸前结法界定印；结跏趺坐于束腰仰覆莲座上。佛像腿部与莲花座相接处有残缺，锈蚀。

The seat is 4.5 cm in height, the figure is 15.2 cm in height, the width is 6.7 cm. The

Buddha has a topknot and small snail-shell curls on his head, which is decorated with beads in between. He is wearing a cassock on the upper body with his right shoulder bared, and a shawl covering both shoulders. His two hands are tied in front of the chest to make a mudra, and he is sitting with legs crossed on the lotus seat. Part of the Buddha's legs is damaged and rusted at the junction with the seat.

18. 清铜鎏金佛像
Gilded bronze Buddha statue, the Qing Dynasty

座高3.7厘米，像高12.1厘米，宽8厘米。佛像挽高髻，头戴五叶花冠；眉间有白毫，双眼微闭；胸前挂长璎珞悬垂至腹部，臂、腕、足均佩戴璎珞；着袒右肩袈裟，下着长裤；双手施法界定印；结跏趺坐于束腰仰覆莲座上。莲台高起，上沿饰一周饱满的连珠纹。通体鎏金。锈蚀。

The seat is 3.7 cm in height, the figure is 12.1 cm in height, the width is 8 cm. Buddha has a topknot on his head, which is decorated with a five-leaf flower crown. He has white hair between the eyebrows, with his eyes slightly closed. He is wearing a jade necklace in front of his chest, which falls to the belly, and jade braces on his arms, artifices and ankles. On his upper body, he is wearing a cassock with his right shoulder bared, and trousers on his legs. His two hands are tied in front of the chest to make a mudra, and he is sitting with crossed legs on the high lotus seat with linked-pearl patterns. The whole statue is gilded, with some part of it rusted.

第三章　金辉玉蕴——金银玉器
The Delicacy of Gold, Silver and Jade Ware

玉文化的内涵丰富。汉代许慎在《说文解字》中说：玉，石之美兼五德者。所谓五德，是指玉的五个特性。凡具有坚韧的质地、晶润的光泽、绚丽的色彩、致密而透明的组织、舒扬致远的声音的美石，都被认为是玉。先秦时代，首饰以珠玉、绿松石为主。汉代至魏晋南北朝，金饰种类逐渐增多。

The jade in Chinese culture has a broader connotation. Xu Shen in the Han Dynasty said in *Shu Wen Jie Zi*, jade has five virtues of stone. The so-called five virtues refer to the five characteristics of jade. All beautiful stones with tough texture, crystalline light, brilliant colors, dense and transparent organization, comfortable and melodious sound are considered jade. In the pre-Qin period, jewelry was mainly made of jade or turquoise. From the Han Dynasty to the Wei, Jin and Southern and Northern Dynasties, various types of gold ornaments increased slightly.

金华素有"小邹鲁"之称，历来为文化礼仪之邦，名人志士众多。新中国成立后，金华出土了许多珍贵文物。1987年，良渚玉璧在双龙洞出土，东阳前山大墓出土众多的玉石器。宋龙首琵琶形青玉带钩及金东区出土的南宋茶具，因其精湛的工艺及历史代表性在台湾地区展出。此外，金华博物馆馆藏的宋、明金银饰品具有典型的时代地域特点。其中，宋银鎏金花头桥梁钗共有19支花头，为目前浙江省花头桥梁钗之冠。20世纪70年代，金华发掘出土了许多明清时期饰件，如金累丝蜜蜂饰、银鎏金凤凰纹发簪、累丝灯笼形金耳环等，其繁复精致程度较为罕见。这些珍贵的玉石、金银器遗存，再次证明了婺州是古越文明的重要组成部分。

Jinhua is known as "Little Zoulu" and has always been a country of cultural etiquette, plenty of celebrities. Many precious cultural relics were unearthed after the founding of the People's Republic of China. Liangzhu Jade Bi was unearthed in the Shuanglong Cave in 1987, numerous jade ware and stone ware were unearthed in Dongyang Qianshan Tomb. The *pipa*-shaped sapphire belt with the design of a dragon head of the Song Dynasty and the tea set of the Southern Song Dynasty unearthed in Jindong District were exhibited in Chinese Taiwan region, for their exquisite craftsmanship and historical representativeness. In addition, the Song and Ming gold and silver jewelries stored in the Jinhua Museum have typical characteristics of time and region. Among them, the Song silver gilded hairpins with gold flowers and bridges have 19 bridges, which is the most in Zhejiang Province. In the 1970s, many ornaments from the Ming and Qing Dynasties were unearthed, such as gold wired bee-shaped ornament, the hairpins with the design of silver gilded golden phoenix and the golden earrings with the design of lanterns, whose complexity and refinement are rare. The remains of these precious jade, gold and silver vessels once again prove that Wuzhou is an important component of the ancient Yue civilization.

1. 良渚玉璧

Liangzhu *yubi* (a jade disc)

该器外径8.7厘米，内径3.6厘米，厚0.4厘米，1991年出土于金华双龙洞。通体素面无纹，钙化严重呈粉白色。

It was 8.7 cm in the external diameter, 3.6 cm in the internal diameter, and 0.4 cm in thickness. It was unearthed in Jinhua Shuanglong Cave in 1991. The surface is plain without lines, and is pink white because of the severe calcification.

璧是一种中央穿孔的扁平状圆形玉器，为我国传统的玉礼器之一，也是"六瑞"之一，体现了贵族对财富的占有。古文献中首次提到玉璧的作用是在《周礼》，"以玉作六器，以礼天地四方：以苍璧礼天，以黄琮礼地，以青圭礼东方，以赤璋礼南方，以白琥礼西方，以玄璜礼北方。"从此玉璧被定为礼器，体现了其在祭祀中的首要地位。

Bi is a flat round jade with a perforation in center. It is one of the traditional jade ritual vessels in our country and one of the "Six Rui (six auspicious items)", which reflects the possession of wealth by the nobility. The role of jade bi was firstly mentioned in the ancient literature *Zhouli*, saying, "in the rituals, using jade to make six artifacts to gift the Heaven and the Earth; using *cangbi* to gift the Heaven, *huangcong* to the Earth, *qinggui* to the East, *chizhang* to the South, *baihu* to the West and *xuanhuang* to the North". Since then, *yubi* was designated as a ritual vessel, embodying the primacy of sacrifice.

2. 宋海棠式玉环
Cherry-apple shaped jade ring, the Song Dynasty

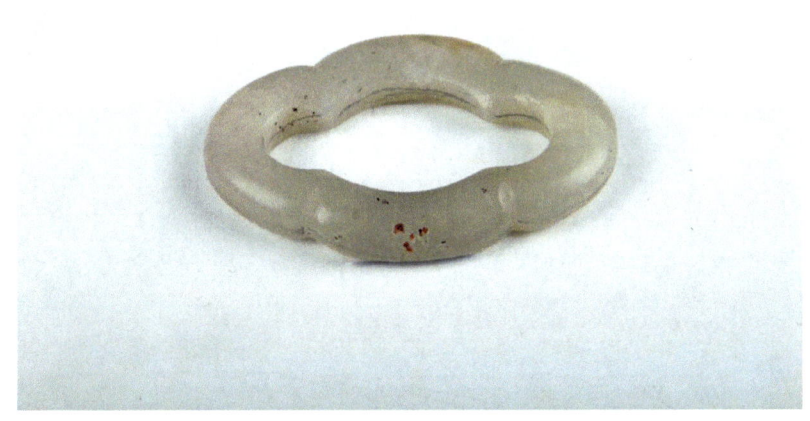

该器长6.2厘米，宽4厘米，厚0.7厘米。青白玉，玉质温润细腻，呈海棠式环状。线条柔美，器表素面无纹。疑为绦环，作佩饰之用。

The ring is 6.2 cm in length, 4 cm in width and 0.7 cm in thickness. It is made by smooth bluish-white jade, and takes the shape of the cherry-apple flower with an elegant curve. The ring is not decorated with any patterns on the surface, and it is believed to be a silk ribbon ring to be used as an accessory.

宋代文人穿着闲居之服时，腰间系丝绦，下端缀流苏，并常用绦环来括结这根丝绦。宋代绦环多以玉石制成，所谓"清其意而洁其身"。宋代海棠式玉绦环形状独特，线条柔和，佩于腰间时与分垂两边的丝绦相得益彰，尽显文人之风流。

When the literati in the Song Dynasty wore leisurely clothes, around their waist, they tied a silk ribbon whose end was decorated with tassels. The silk braid was often used to tie a jade ring. In the Song Dynasty, the ring was mostly made of jade, standing for being clean and pure. This piece of relic has a unique shape and soft lines. When worn around the waist, it complements the silk ribbons hanging on both sides, which fully demonstrates the literati's romance.

3. 宋龙首琵琶形青玉带钩
Green jade *pipa*-shaped belt hook with the design of a dragon head, the Song Dynasty

该器长12厘米，宽3.5厘米，高2.6厘米。它是一种古代生活用品。1994年6月，南宋郑继道家族墓出土。该器为青色玉质。钩体为扭曲S型，长把短钩作龙首状，腹作琵琶形，下有圆柱，近于一端，柱顶圆形。

It is 12 cm in length, 3.5 cm in width and 2.6 cm in height. It is a household utensil in ancient times, which was unearthed in the tomb of Zheng Jidao family in Jinhua in June, 1994. The green jade, takes the shape of a twisted S. It has a long handle and a short hook with the design of a dragon head, and the belly of it resembles the shape of a *pipa*, underneath which is a pillar with a round bottom.

该器局部有星星点点的白色水沁。龙首雕刻精巧，眼鼻十分紧凑，眼睛为圆柱形突出，龙首的眉毛上扬，相向弯转呈勾云纹；眉梢用阴线刻出，向后飘出，眉额隆起，有重眉压眼之感。两角向后微卷，两耳紧贴角下，为水滴形。耳后为长须。龙首的吻部雕刻十分精细，每一颗牙齿都细细雕出。玉带钩造型优美，雕刻精巧，对研究南宋时期金华地区的政治、经济、文化具有一定的历史价值。

Several splashes of water mark disperse on some part of it. The dragon head is well-carved, on which the cylinder eyes embed on the protruding forehead, and carved lines depict the raising eyebrows. The water drop shaped ears of it are attached tightly to the antlers, with long hair at the back of the ears. The mouth of it is also delicate, with every tooth of it clearly carved. The belt is in elegant shape with nice craftsmanship, which is of significance to the study of politics, economy and culture of Jinhua during the Southern Song Dynasty.

4. 宋螭龙纹青白玉璧

Bluish-white dragon-pattern jade, the Song Dynasty

该器直径8.1厘米，孔径3.1厘米，璧宽2.5厘米，厚1厘米。青白玉，玉璧周缘起棱，其两面均雕刻精细螭龙纹。正面的三条螭龙首尾相接；反面为浅雕三条螭龙纹，形态各异。

The object is 8.1 cm in overall diameter, 3.1 cm in diameter at the inner hole, 2.5 cm in the width of the ring and 1 cm in thickness. It is made of bluish-white jade, with ridges on the edge of it, and delicate patterns of a dragon on the surface of both sides. The front side is carved three vivid dragons connected end to end, while the backside is decorated with three dragons of different shaping.

5. 宋扣金如意头形料器碟
Golden plate with a design of *ruyi*, the Song Dynasty

该器长8.7厘米、宽7.2厘米、高1.6厘米。它出土于金东区东孝街道陶朱路城北公园工地。造型为椭圆如意头形，折沿，圜底。口沿镶扣金质镂空錾花卷草珠点图案，边缘焊粟金珠。它是古代的一种酒器，名为曲卮。此器造型典雅，雕刻精美华丽。

The object is 8.7 cm in length, 7.2 cm in width and 1.6 cm in height. It unearthed at the construction site of Chengbei Park, Taozhu Road, Dongxiao Sub-district, Jindong District. It takes the shape of an oval with *ruyi*-shaped fringe, folded rim and a surrounded bottom. The rim of it is decorated with golden patterns of hollowed-out flowers and plants, connected to a smooth surface tinted with grey. It is a type of wine container, being called Quzhi. This instrument is elegant in shape and beautifully carved.

6. 宋金指铤

Golden chain of rings, the Song Dynasty

　　该器直径1.7厘米，高1.6厘米。纯金质，缠钏式，通体光素无纹。指铤头用粗丝缠作活环，与下层的连环套接，可以通过左右滑动来调节松紧。

　　It is 1.7 cm in diameter, and 1.6 cm in height. It is made by pure gold, and takes the shape of a coil with no decorations at all. The top of the rings is made into a slipknot by thick thread, which is connected to the chains of rings below and can be adjusted by slipping.

　　指铤多见于南宋，为聘礼中的"三金"之一。南宋吴自牧《梦粱录·卷二十·嫁娶》中记载："且论聘礼，富贵之家当备三金送之，则金钏、金铤、金帔坠者是也。"

　　The chains of rings were common in the Southern Song Dynasty, and had been one of the three gifts in betrothal presents. *Menglianglu. Volume Twenty. the Marriage* written by Wu Zimu of the Southern Song Dynasty records that "in terms of betrothal presents, the rich and noble family should prepare three gold items — gold bracelet, gold anklet and gold pendant."

7. 宋镂花金梳背
Gold comb-back ornament with engraved designs, the Song Dynasty

该器为纯金质，半月形。在顶部相连的半月形金片上，由金丝掐制成的梅花焊接在梳背的两端，中间用炸珠焊接工艺将金珠焊接在梳背上，呈连珠（珍珠）纹，且纹饰极其细密。器身中空，以插梳齿。

It is pure gold with a half-moon shape. On the half-moon-shaped gold piece connected at the top, the plum blossoms made of gold wire were welded to the two ends of the comb back, and the gold beads were welded to the comb back by the deep-fried bead welding technology in the middle, showing a continuous bead (pearl) pattern. The pattern is extremely fine. The body is hollow, easy for inserting comb teeth.

宋时插梳十分风行，稍微有身份的年轻女子均头戴冠或插梳，且插戴位置前后均可。所谓"梳背儿"，是指梳脊包金或包银的木梳，这是宋元以来的传统做法。扬之水先生将宋人梳背的特点总结为：与唐代相比，在形制上的不同是装饰带由半月形易作虹桥形，并且多半是因梳背与梳栉质地不同而分别制作。常见的类型为虹桥式装饰带，其装饰方面以金银片作包镶为主。

Wearing combs was very popular in the Song Dynasty. Young women with slight respect wore crowns or combs in front or at back on their heads. The so-called "comb-back ornaments" referred to a wooden comb covered with gold or silver on its comb spine, which was a tradition since the Song and Yuan Dynasties. Mr. Yang Zhishui summarized the characteristics of the comb-back ornaments of the Song people as follows: Compared with the Tang Dynasty, the decorative belt was changed from a half-moon shape to a rainbow bridge shape, for the combs had different comb backs and comb raw materials. The most common type was the rainbow-bridge-styled belt, which was mainly decorated with gold and silver pieces.

8. 明双耳玉杯
Jade cup with double ears, the Ming Dynasty

该玉杯底径4厘米，口径9厘米，为饮酒器。青白玉质，圆形敞口，圈足，附龙形双耳，器身浮雕莲瓣纹一周，刻工精细，造型优美。玉杯称"玉栮"，亦称"玉盉"，是玉制的杯的美称。

The cup is 4 cm in diameter at bottom rim, and 9 cm in diameter at top rim. It is a drinking vessel, made of blue and white jade, with round opening mouth, ringed feet and dragon-shaped double ears, and it was embossed lotus petals on the body, which is finely carved and beautiful in shape. "*Yubei*" in Chinese characters of "玉杯" is also called "玉梧" or "玉盉", a beautiful addressing of jade cups.

9. 明银鎏金凤纹发簪
The hairpins with the design of silver gilded golden phoenix, the Ming Dynasty

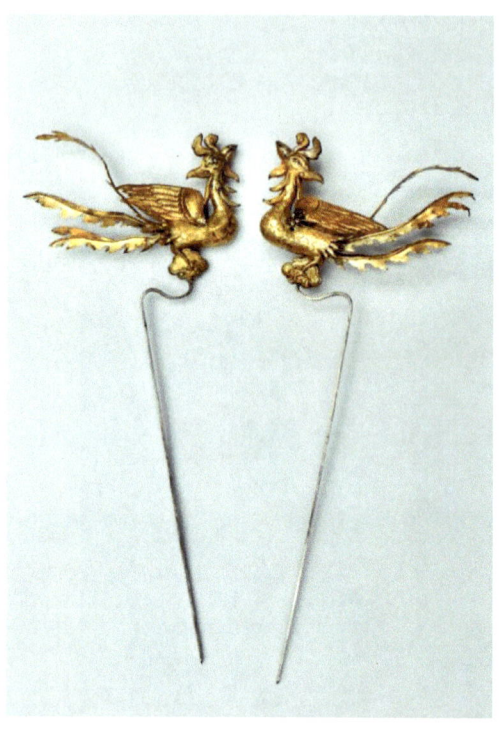

这组凤簪共两件，全器分件铸造，再金焊而成。簪头为银鎏金凤，将翅膀、尾部以焊接工艺组成立体的凤。凤立在一朵祥云之上，显得雍容华贵。凤足与簪身相连。明代女子金银首饰纳于礼仪制度，一等的是凤冠霞帔，插在凤冠上的便是一对金凤簪，作固定凤冠之用。

There are two pieces of phoenix hairpins in this group, which were all cast separately and then welded by gold. The hairpin is a silver gilded phoenix whose wings and tail are welded to form a three-dimensional phoenix. The phoenix stands above the auspicious cloud, being graceful and luxurious. The phoenix feet are connected to the hairpin body. Women's gold and silver jewelries in the Ming Dynasty were included in the etiquette system. The women of the first class wore the phoenix coronet and robes of rank. One pair of golden phoenix hairpins inserted on the phoenix coronet was used to fix it.

10. 清累丝灯笼形金耳环
Golden earrings with the design of lanterns, the Qing Dynasty

该耳环长7.1厘米，宽2厘米。金质，灯笼形。耳坠集掐丝、累丝、捶打、錾刻、焊接等多种工艺精制而成。装饰的上方是一个五爪提系，提系顶端为圆环，五爪之端有五个金累丝的云钩，提系下边接焊一顶金累丝花朵式伞盖。伞盖下坠金累丝透空花球样宫灯与用金丝编结成的镂空六角形宫灯，中间以圆环相连。六角形宫灯下端用金丝编结成灯座，可谓玲珑之至。

The object is 7.1 cm in length and 2 cm in width, which is made by pure gold and takes the shape of a lantern. The earrings were well made after procedures such as pinching, bundling, hammering, carving and welding. At the top of the decorations is a loop of design of five paws, top of which is a round ring and a hook made by gold. Under the loop is a flower shaped cap made by golden threads to be followed by a spherical lantern and a hexagon lantern, which are combined by a ring in the middle. Underneath the hexagon lantern is a delicate lamp stand made by knitting the gold threads.

第四章　翰墨文心——书画
Ingenious Paintings and Calligraphy

中国书画源远流长，考古发掘的中国最早的绘画形式有岩画和刻绘、彩陶纹饰、地画、壁画与帛画等。唐宋以来，绘画形式多为用毛笔蘸水、墨、彩作画于绢或纸上，题材分为人物、山水、花鸟等，技法分为具象和写意。在内容和艺术创作上，它体现了古人对自然、社会及与之相关联的政治、哲学、宗教、道德、文学等方面的认知。

Chinese painting and calligraphy have a long history. The earliest forms of Chinese painting discovered through archaeological excavations include rock paintings and carvings, colored pottery patterns, floor paintings, murals and silk paintings. Since the Tang and Song Dynasties, brushes dipped in water, ink and paint were used to paint on silk or paper generally. The subjects included figures, landscapes, flowers and birds, etc. The techniques could be divided into concrete and freehand brushwork. In terms of content and artistic creation, it reflects the ancient people's cognition of nature, society and related politics, philosophy, religion, morality, literary, and other aspects.

明清时期是中国绘画史上较为繁盛的时代，金华因其历史悠久、文人辈出、书画氛围甚浓，而产生了以金华籍名士杜鳌、姜岱、王备为代表的南方指画流派。其与北方高其佩所倡导的指画交相辉映，影响深远。著名画家黄宾虹、潘天寿、蒋莲僧、张书旂、吴弗之等均有指墨画遗世，现金华博物馆馆藏指墨画传承有序，艺术性颇高。

Ming and Qing Dynasties were a prosperous era in the history of Chinese painting. Jinhua because of its long history, large numbers of literati and a strong atmosphere of calligraphy and painting, gave birth to the southern finger painting school dominated by famous Jinhua celebrities — Du Ao, Jiang Dai, and Wang Bei. It complements the finger paintings advocated by Gao Qipei in the north, and has a profound impact. Famous painters such as Huang Binhong, Pan Tianshou, Jiang Lianseng, Zhang Shuqi and Wu Fuzhi all have finger-ink paintings. The current collected finger-ink paintings in Jinhua museum has an orderly inheritance and high artistic quality.

此外，金华深厚的文化艺术积蕴吸引了一部分擅长丹青的文人墨客来婺州交流学习，他们留下了许多优秀的书画作品。如描绘清中期金华地理环境、城池建制的《金华府城图》，黄宾虹与客居金华的师友汪达川关于《画论》的书函等。金华博物馆馆藏的218幅明清扇面精品中，更不乏王宠、彭年、张宏、陆治、任薰等大家之作。此外，博物馆还收藏了数十方印章，其中一枚为民国时期白文"龙渊印社"青田石方章，为其首任社长金维坚所刻。龙渊印社诞生于抗日烽火之中。从创社伊始，它就有着鲜明的艺术主张和风格，其朴茂、刚健的篆刻风格与国家危亡之际民众奋起抗争的时代精神相一致。首创社团中有数位金华人，这对研究金华近现代印学发展史有重要意义。

In addition, the profound cultural and artistic accumulation has attracted a large number of scholars who are good at painting came to Wuzhou (Jinhua) for exchange and study, leaving many excellent paintings and calligraphy works for Jinhua. For example, there is *The Map of Jinhua Prefecture*, depicting the geographical environment and organization system of Jinhua in the middle of the Qing Dynasty; there are letters on *Painting Theory* from Huang Binhong and his mentor Wang Dachuan who sojourned in Jinhua. Among the 218 fine Ming and Qing fans, there are many works painted by Wang Chong, Peng Nian, Zhang Hong, Lu Zhi, Ren Xun and others. In addition, the museum also houses dozens of seals, one of which is the Qingtian stone seal with characters of "Longyuan Yinshe (Longyuan Seal Association)" of the Republic of China carved by its first president, Jin Weijian. Longyuan Yinshe was born in the period of the anti-Japanese war. From the very beginning, it has had distinct artistic propositions and style advocacy. Its simple and robust seal cutting style was consistent with the spirit of the times when the country was in peril. Several of the pioneer clubs are all from Jinhua, which is of great significance to the study of the development history of Jinhua's modern seal.

自宋以来，浙江成为全国四大刻书中心之一，金华作为南宋陪都，不仅文化得到了长足发展，而且婺州刻书业更是异军突起。不少冠绝一时的婺刻珍本，更是对中国的文化传播产生了一定的影响。

Since the Song Dynasty, Zhejiang has been one of the four major book-engraving centers in the country. Jinhua, as the companion capital of the Southern Song Dynasty, has not only made great progress in its culture, but also the book-engraving industry. Many of the most rare Wu (Jinhua) carved books have had a certain impact on the spread of Chinese culture.

丽泽书院本、吴氏祠堂本、唐宅刊本、州学郡斋本等，字体遒劲，别具风格，其中以我国最早的画谱《梅花喜神谱》二卷、《切韵指掌图》二卷、《周礼注》十二卷、《欧阳先生文粹》二十卷、《圣宋文选》三十二卷、《东莱吕太史文集》十五卷等最为珍稀。元明清的婺州刻书印书，虽不及宋之盛，但其书脉仍延续。明著名版本有《宋学士文粹》、《金华文统》十三卷等。清永康胡凤丹从《四库全书存目》中辑唐至清金华先贤著作165篇，刻鸿篇大著《金华丛书》，共67种340册。其子胡宗懋增刻《续金华丛书》58种。民国时期《双龙纪胜》装帧精美、图文并茂，代表当时出版物的最高水准。

The books engraved and printed in places like Lize Academy, Wu's Ancestral Hall, Tangzhai and Zhouxue junzhai had strong and unique styles. The earliest painting book—2 volumes of *Meihua Xishen Pu*, 2 volumes of *Qieyun Zhizhang Tu*, 12 volumes of *Zhoulizhu*, 20 volumes of *Ouyang Xiansheng Wencui*, 32 volumes of *Shengsong Wenxuan* and 15 volumes of *Donglai Lvtaishi Wenji* are the most rare. Although the engraving and printing of books in Wuzhou in the Yuan, Ming and Qing Dynasties was not as good as in the peak period of the Song Dynasty, its history still continued. Famous editions of the Ming Dynasty include *Song Xue Shi Wen Cui*, 13 volumes of *Jin Hua Wen Tong*. Hu Fengdan of Yongkang of the Qing Dynasty compiled *Jinhua Serious I* from *Siku Quanshu Cunmu* which selected 165 masterpieces written by sages of Jinhua from the Tang Dynasty to the Qing Dynasty. *The Jinhua Series I* has 340 books in 67 varieties. His son Hu Zongmao compiled *Jinhua Series II* in 58 varieties. *Shuanglong Jisheng* at the period of the Republic of China was beautifully decorated with pictures and texts, representing the highest level of publications at that time.

1. 明张瑞图书法册页

Zhang Ruitu's calligraphy albums, the Ming Dynasty

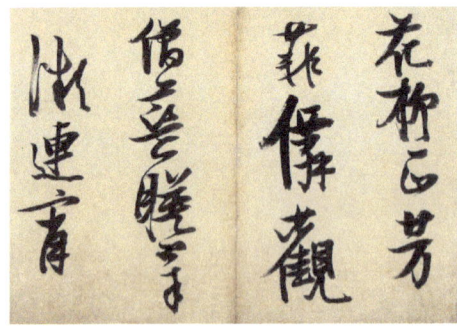 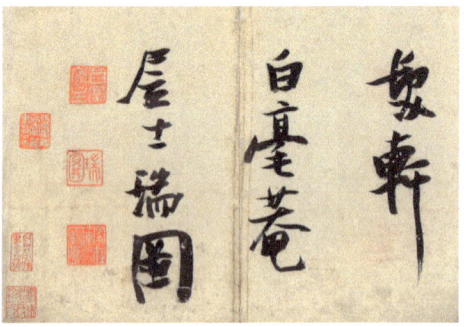

该作品纵25厘米，横36.5厘米；内文为绢，前后题跋为纸；写于明崇祯五年（1632年）。

It is 25 cm in width, 36.5 cm in length. The material for writing main text is silk, and for preface and postscript is paper. It was written in the fifth year of Chongzheng, the Ming Dynasty (1632).

题签：《白毫庵主墨迹》，全文为行草《燕子矶放歌》，共分20张（每张折页不连）。

The album of 20 separate pieces is titled with *Baihao Superior's Calligraphy*, and its content is *Sing Aloud at Yanziji* with running script through the full text.

跋:"崇祯壬申秋中书于东湖之晞发轩白毫庵居士瑞图"。

Postscript: "Written by Baihao Superior Ruitu at Xifa Pavilion of East Lake in Autumn on Chongzheng Renshen".

第一序文为行楷,光绪丁酉夏五月。

The first preface was written in running-regular script and completed in the May of Guangxu Dingyou.

第二序文为行楷,在岁乙未年,由叶新第书。

The second preface was written by Ye Xindi in running-regular script at the end of Yiwei Year.

尾跋文为行书,丙辰仲夏,由章景枫书。

The postscript was written by Zhang Jingfeng in running script at the mid-summer of Bingchen Year.

钤印:瑞图(朱文),白毫庵主(白文)。

Stamp: Ruitu (Red), Baihao Superior (White).

收藏印:张庸畅真赏,张庸畅印,桐城庄氏珍玩,石夫鉴赏(朱文);
张庸畅所宝法书名画,家在莲花岛,有宋少师之裔(白文)。

Stamps of collectors: True Connoisseurship by Zhang Yongchang, Zhang Yongchang's Stamp, Rare Curios of the Zhuang's, Tongcheng, Appreciated by Shifu (Red).

Zhang Yongchang Valuable Calligraphy and Painting, Live at Lianhua Island, Offspring of Song Shaoshi (White).

张瑞图(1570—1644年),字长公、无画,号二水、白毫庵主、白毫庵主道人等。晋江二十七都下行乡(福建省晋江市青阳下行乡)人。明万历三十五年探花,授翰林院编修,后以礼部尚书入阁,晋建极殿大学士。明代四大书法家之一,与董其昌、邢侗、米万钟齐名,有"南张北董"之号。他擅长山水画,效法元代黄公望,画风苍劲,作品传世极稀。此书法册页,笔墨奇逸,峻峭劲利,笔势生动,姿态横生,实为佳作。

Zhang Ruitu (1570—1644), whose courtesy name was Changgong or Wuhua, also self-titled Ershui, or Baihao Superior, or Baihao Superior Daoist, born in

Xiaxing County, Twenty-seven City, Jinjiang(Xiaxing County, Qingyang, Jinjiang, Fujian). He achieved the third place in the imperial examination in the 35th year of Wanli Period, the Ming Dynasty, and was appointed to compile and edit at Imperial Academy, later promoted to the cabinet as Grand Secretary of Hall of Jianji. As one of four famous calligrapher in the Ming Dynasty, he was on a par with Dong Qichang, Xing Dong and Mi Wanzhong, reputed as "Master Zhang in the southern China, while Master Dong in the northern China". He excelled in landscape painting and followed the paintings of Huang Gongwang in the Yuan Dynasty. His works were painted vigorously, but very few was left. This calligraphy albums was painted unconventionally and powerfully. The vivid and picturesque painting made it a fine piece of work.

2. 明宾月楼图咏手卷

Binyue building illustrated book hand scroll, the Ming Dynasty

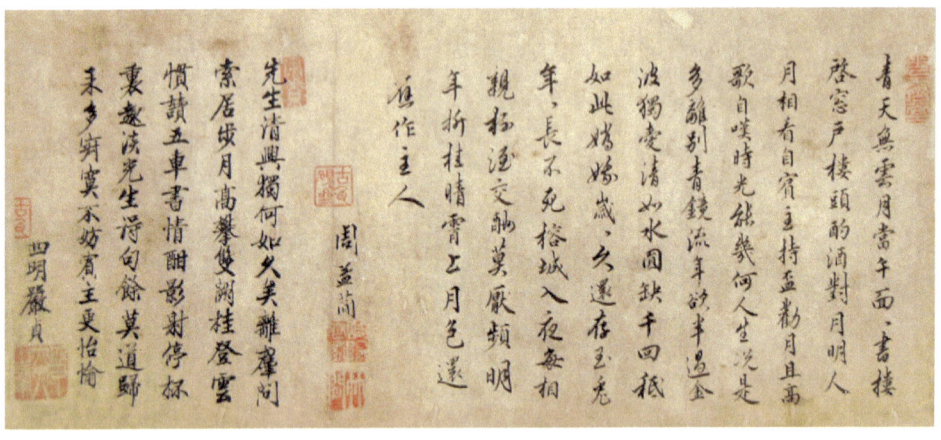

该作品长 1 077.5 厘米，高 24 厘米；画心为绢，跋为纸；题跋为明永乐、宣德、天启及清至民国时期名人题记数篇。

It is 1,077.5 cm in length, 24 cm in width; the material for painting main text is silk, and for postscript is paper. The postscripts were written by the scholars from different dynasties like Yongle, the Ming Dynasty, Xuande, Tianqi, the Qing Dynasty and the Republic of China period.

题签：《宾月楼图卷》乙卯仲秋金华章景枫题签。

Book title: *Binyue Building Illustrated Book* wrote by Zhang Jingfeng at Jinhua in the mid-autumn, 1945.

题头：《宾月》潓士。

Title: *Binyue* Unsecularized Literati.

题头钤印：金门大隐（白文），古瓦（朱文），神品（白文），梁章钜审定书画之印（白文）。

Stamp for the title: Jinmendayin (white), Guwa (red), Shenpin (white), Calligraphy and Painting Evaluated by Liang Zhangju Stamp (white).

画面款识：宾月楼图。拱北观同年曾收得明人宾月楼图卷子，只余后题跋，茹则图不知何人所作，已无存矣，属余补成之草草，应命未谂于原题跋有合否尔，乙卯八月大雄山民弟姜筠并识。

The inscription: Binyue Building Painting Gongbeiguan. In the same year, the Binyue Building illustrated book of some person in the Ming Dynasty was collected, but only its postscript was remained. I didn't know the painter of the Ruze painting which was lost. I roughly painted one and didn't know whether it fitted the original postscript or not. Daxiongshanmin Jiang Yun inscribed his name on it on August, 1945.

画面钤印：姜筠之印（白文），大雄山民（白文）。

Stamp on the painting: Jiang Yun's Stamp (white), Daxiongshanmin (white).

姜筠（1847—1919 年），字颖生，别号大雄山民，安徽怀宁人，官礼部主事。山水专学王翚，笔法浓重，间作花卉，兼喜篆刻。此卷为姜筠因友人得明人宾月楼卷题跋后补画的"宾月楼图"。题跋因有明永乐、宣德、天启及清至民国时期名人题记数篇，字迹清秀隽永，故甚为珍贵。

Jiang Yun (1847—1919), whose courtesy name was Yingsheng, also self-titled Daxiongshanmin, born in Huaining Anhui, worked as Director of the Board of Rites. He learned landscape painting after Wang Hui with strong brush-working. Sometimes, he would paint flowers and plants, and also liked seal cutting. Based on the postscript of Binyue Building scroll of a Ming person obtained by his friend, he painted this "Binyue Building Painting". The postscript included the elegant writings of the scholars from Yongle, the Ming Dynasty, Xuande, Tianqi, the Qing Dynasty and the Republic of China period, deserves to be called as the precious work.

3. 清拓明万历孙讷刊金刚经塔刻石拓片轴
Carved scroll of Jing Gangjing in the Qing Dynasty by Sun Ne during Wanli Period of Ming Dynasty

纸本。右上角题：金则经塔，董其昌书。落款："万历己亥长至日，宫保陆树声。"施刊者多为名公大佬：唐文献、顾正心、陆彦章、俞汝楫、徐继溥、钟允善、徐曾孙、殷之仪、薛九思、万惟智、薛文焕、计应科、叶鸣国、陈继儒、陈缙儒。弟子孙讷刻。

Paper painting. The title on the top right corner: Jinzejing Tower, written by Dong Qichang. Signature:"the summer solstice of the 27th year of Wanli, Gongbao (tutor to the crown prince) Lu Shusheng." Most poets were the celebrities: Tang Wenxian, Gu Zhengxin, Lu Yanzhang, Yu Ruji, Xu Jipu, Zhong Yunshan, Xu Zengsun, Yin Zhiyi, Xue Jiusi, Wan Weizhi, Xue Wenhuan, Ji Yingke, Ye

Mingguo, Chen Jiru, Chen Jinru. Carved by Student Sun Ne.

  拓片为满布经文的一座七级浮图，顶有塔刹，每层檐角悬铃一对。除第四层之外，每层各有一身坐佛，此坐佛，恰作经文中的"佛"字读。第四层的中央是一座塔，又刚好是在经文的"皆知供养如佛塔庙"处，"佛"字与"庙"字之间的这座塔，便作经文中的"塔"字读。第一层，门内佛陀说法，佛陀十大弟子"解空第一"之须菩提跪听，门外两侧各一身金刚卫士。门楣自左向右书《金刚般若波罗蜜经》，塔门内侧，佛左方是经文起始"如是我闻，一时，佛在舍卫城……"，佛右方"皆大欢喜，信受奉行"，是经文之结束。而"金"与结末之"行"字相接，"经"与起首之"如"字相衔，首尾并对，起结贯通。此镌刻于七层宝塔的《金刚经》，精妙特之处在于其布算安排，栏杆、柱子、斗棋、瓦垄、屋脊、铃铎、塔刹，经文满填无馀，依形回旋，而起结对应，宛若天成。

  The rubbing depicted a seven-tiered pagoda with a tower spire on its top and a pair of bells hanging on the corner of every floor. Expect for the forth floor, a sitting Buddha was placed in each floor. The pronunciation of this sitting Buddha was the same as the "Buddha (fo)" in the scriptures. A tower was placed in the middle of the forth floor, where was the place like the pagoda (Fo Ta Miao) to offer tributes. The ta (tower) was pronounced as the "ta" in the scriptures. Inside the first floor, there was a Buddha expounding Buddhist doctrine inside. Xuputi, one of ten students of the Buddha, reputed as "Jie Kong Di Yi" was listening to the Buddha on his knees. Each side outside the door stood a vajra bodyguard. *The Diamond Sutra: The Perfection of Wisdom* (Jin Gang Bo Re Bo Luo Mi Jing) was written on the lintel from left to right. The inside of the tower door, namely the left side of the Buhhda, was written on the start of the scriptures "I heard that, Buhhda Sakyamuni was at Shewei (Ru Shi Wo Wen, Yi Shi, Fo Zai She Wei Cheng)", on the right was written "Everyone learn satisfyingly and act to practice (Jie Da Huan Xi, Xin Shou Feng Xing)", the end of the scriptures. The character "Jin" connected with the character "Xing", while the character "Jing" connected with the character "Ru", which made a cohesive connection. The delicacy of this *Jin Gang Jing* carved on seven-tiered tower lied in its overall arrangement. All the railings, pillars, *douqi*, rows of tiles on roof, ridge, bells under palace eaves and tower spire were covered with scriptures, which was carved along the shape of building and made a natural cohesive connection.

4. 清乾隆四十六年姜岱指墨山水轴

Jiang Dai's landscape scroll, the 46th year of Qianlong, the Qing Dynasty

该作品纵154厘米，横91厘米；纸本；画于1781年。

It is 154 cm in width, 91 cm in length; paper scroll; this finger painting landscape painted scroll is completed in 1781.

款识：群峰叠叠耸高秋/云外山泉水飞流/忆昔铜岩岭（台山）上遇/写来狂记应时游。

Inscription: Overlapped peaks tower into the clouds in the autumn, while outside the clouds rushes the spring. On recalling the encounter in the Tongyan Mountain, I hereby write excitedly to record the tour in season.

钤印：臣姜岱印（白文）；

大学校书（朱文）。

Stamp: Jiang Dai's stamp (white);

Da Xue Jiao Shu (red).

姜岱，字仰山，金华仁义里人，擅长指画、书法、诗，尤以画八哥闻名。他是杜鳌的弟子，其指画作品清时在浙江颇有知名度，现代书画大师黄宾虹、潘天寿也受其画法的启发和影响。乾隆南巡时曾亲自御览其画，极为赞赏。其作品曾收录于《墨香居画识》。该画气势磅礴，画面右上方两边山石夹一大瀑布顺流而下，瀑布下方，云雾缭绕，一丛树木从旁斜出，画中的一方岩石上有二人似在观瀑布。该作品指法娴熟，气势宏大，虚实相宜，动静相呼。

Jiang Dai, whose courtesy name was Yang Shan, born in Renyili, Jinhua, excelled in finger painting, calligraphy, poem writing, especially famous for painting mynah. As the student of Du Ao, he was well-known for his finger painting at Zhejiang in the Qing Dynasty. His painting style and skills also influenced and inspired modern calligraphy and painting masters Huang Binhong and Pan Tianshou. During the journey to the south, Emperor Qianlong personally saw his painting and thought highly of them. *Moxiangju Huashi* was collected by descendants. This grand and magnificent painting depicted that, on the top right corner, a great waterfall fell straight from the gorge. Below the waterfall, mist-shrouded, some trees tilted to stretch out. On a stone were two people seemingly appreciated the waterfall. His skillful fingering created a painting of powerful magnificence and proper balance between action and silence.

5. 清乾隆四十七年王备指墨松鹤图轴

Wang Bei's Pine Crane Finger Painting Painted Scroll, the 47th year of Qianlong, the Qing Dynasty

该作品纵163.5厘米，横93厘米；纸本；画于1782年。

It is 163.5 cm in length, 93 cm in width; paper scroll. Pine Crane Finger Painting Painted Scroll was completed in 1782.

款识：乾隆壬寅仲春日，婺城王备指墨。

Inscription: February Renyin, Qianlong, Wang Bei's Finger Painting in Wucheng.

钤印：王备之印（白文），仲周（朱文）。

Stamp: Wang Bei's stamp (white), Zhong Zhou (red).

王备，浙江金华人，清初杜鳌、姜岱金华指画派的代表画家。该作品为指墨画作，画面构图以白鹤为中心，松树为辅。他以指为笔，技法娴熟精练。松鹤羽毛的局部施以薄白粉，渲染了羽毛的质感，多变的指法使白鹤的神态跃然纸上。又以淡指墨写松枝，枯墨点苔，虚实相间，郁郁葱葱，刚柔相济。留白以为云霭雾气，几簇松枝点缀，画面层次鲜明，显得生机勃勃。

Wang Bei, born in Jinhua, Zhejiang, was the representative painter of Du Ao & Jiang Dai Jinhua finger painting school in the early Qing Dynasty. This work was a finger painting, mainly focusing on the crane, and partially on the pine. He skillfully used his fingers as the brush. Some white power was applied to the part of the feathers of the crane through different fingerings to lighten the texture of the feather, making the crane full of life. Pine branches were painted by light-color finger painting, and dried ink was used to paint moss. Different light and dark colors depicted luxuriantly green combining vigor and suppleness. White spaces acted as clouds and mists, decorated by a few pine branches, making a well-arranged and vivid painting.

6. 清光绪二十六年蒲华墨竹四条屏
Pu Hua's black bamboo four pieces painting, the 26th year of Guangxu, the Qing Dynasty

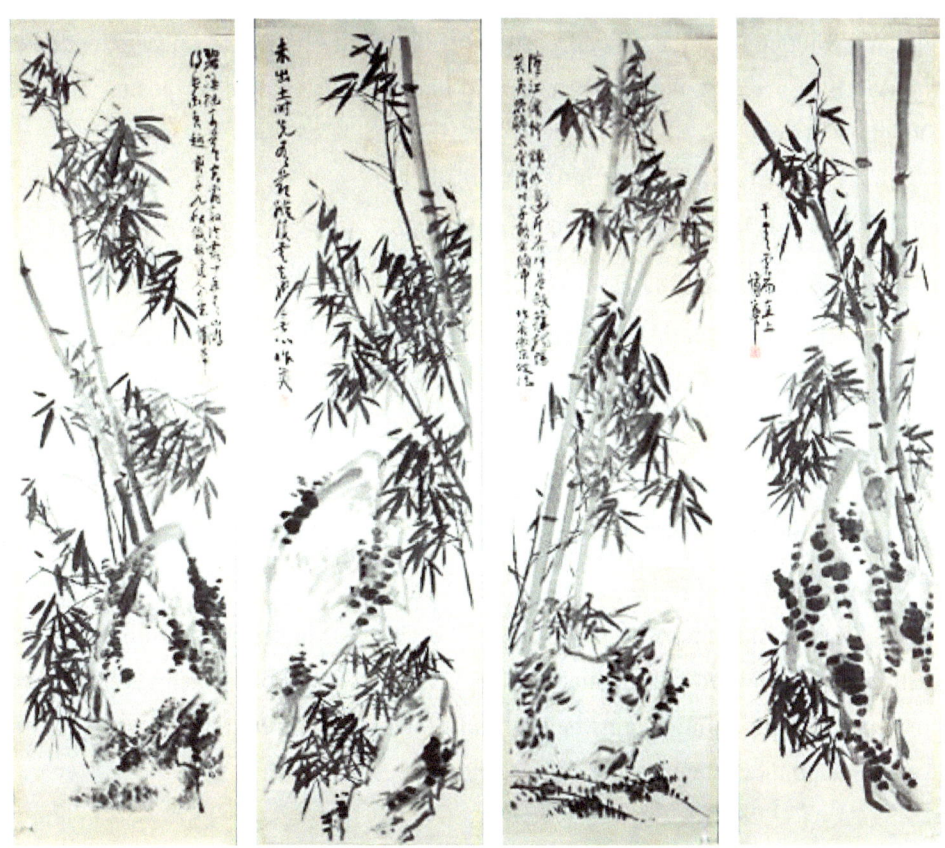

该作品长238厘米，宽60厘米；纸本；写意墨竹，画于1900年。

It is 238 cm in length, 60 cm in width; paper scroll. This freehand black bamboo painting was completed in 1900.

右一款识：干青云而直上，蒲华。

The first inscription on the right: Straight up to the sky Pu Hua.

钤印：作英（白文）。

Stamp: Zuoying (white).

右二款识：汉江修竹贱如蓬，斤斧何曾赦箨龙？堪笑吴兴馋太守，渭川千亩在胸中。作英仿东坡法。

The second inscription on the right: The bamboos in Hanjiang are as cheap as grass, as they have never been exempted from the chop with axes. It was ridiculous that Wu Xing coveted the official position of Prefecture but could only pretended to thousands of acres of Weihe River area in his mind. Zuoying's script that imitates Dongpo's Style.

钤印：秀水蒲华作英（朱文）。

Stamp: Xiushui Pu Hua Zuoying（red）.

右三款识：未出土时先有节，破凌云去也无心。作英。

The third inscription on the right: Born with joints before breaking through the grounds, they will remain hollow though chasing through the clouds. Zuoying.

钤印：蒲华印信（白文）。

Stamp: Pu Hua's Stamp (white).

右四款识：碧筱挺奇节，空霏散冷露。十年春山游，得此幽贞趣。庚子秋拟梅道人大人意。蒲华。

The forth inscription on the right: The Green Bamboos stand upright with distinctive joints when falling thick and fast with cold dew. For ten years, I have been for spring outings in mountains before I appreciated such eremitic pleasure. A Draft for Mr.Mei in the Autumn, the Year of Gengzi. Pu Hua.

钤印：蒲作英（朱文）。

Stamp: Pu Zuoying (red).

蒲华（1832—1911年），字作英，亦作竹英、竹云，浙江嘉兴人；号胥山野史、胥山外史、种竹道人。斋名九琴十砚斋、九琴十研楼、芙蓉庵、剑胆琴心室等。晚清著名书画家，与虚谷、吴昌硕、任伯年合称"海派四杰"。他擅花卉、山水，尤擅画竹，有"蒲竹"之誉。此四屏尺幅颇大，且气势磅礴，笔墨淳厚多姿，风韵清健。

Pu Hua (1832—1911), whose courtesy name was Zuoying, also Zhuying, Zhuyun, was born in Jiaxing, Zhejiang. He self-titled as Xu Shan Ye Shi, Xu

Shan Wai Shi, and Zhong Zhu Dao Ren. He named his dwelling place Jiu Qin Shi Yan Zhai, Jiu Qin Shi Yan Lou, Fu Rong An, Jian Dan Qin Xin Shi. As the famous calligrapher and painter in the late Qing Dynasty, he, along with Xugu, Wu Changshuo and Ren Bonian was reputed as "Hai Pai Si Jie". He was adept at painting flowers and plants, and landscape, especially at bamboo, known as "Pu Bamboo". These four pieces were quite large, powerful and magnificent. These were painted in dark ink of diverse shapes to show fresh and vigorous charm.

7. 民国时期张书旂松鹤立轴

Zhang Shuqi's Crane Vertical Scroll, the period of the Republic of China (1912—1949)

该作品长131厘米，宽50厘米；纸本；设色写意花鸟画。

It is 131 cm in length, 50 cm in width; paper scroll; coloring freehand flower and bird painting.

款识：穉翘老先生七秩荣寿，乙亥夏月书旂写于金陵。

Inscription: To celebrate the 70th birthday of Mr.Zhiqiao Written by Shuqi in Summer Yihai at Jinling.

钤印：张书旂铢（白文）；中国传统艺术宜之宝（朱文）。

Stamp:Zhang Shuqi's Stamp (white); Treasure of Traditional Chinese Art (red).

张书旂（1900—1957年），浙江浦江人。他曾任南京中央大学教授，抗日战争期间去美国创办画院，讲学作画，后定居旧金山。他与徐悲鸿、柳子谷三人并称为画坛的"金陵三杰"。画花鸟时，他喜用白粉调和色墨，使画面典雅明丽，颇具现代感。他得到高剑父与吕凤子亲授，形成色、粉与笔墨兼施的清新流丽画风而独具一格，并出版《书旂花鸟集》《张书旂画集》等。此画为张书旂先生为友人贺寿之作，松鹤题材寓意吉祥，用笔干净简练，色彩明快柔和。他喜用白粉调和色墨，尽显其中。

　　Zhang Shuqi (1900—1957) was born in Pujiang, Zhejiang. He was the professor of Nanjing Central University (now known as Nanjing University) and established Art Academy in the United States during the period of the War of Resistance Against Japanese Aggression. He taught student to paint and then settled in San Francisco. He, Xu Beihong and Liu Zigu were reputed as "Three Masters in Jinling" in the painting school. When painting flowers and birds, he liked to use white power to mix with other colors, making his painting elegant, bright and quite modern. Learning from Gao Jianfu and Lv Fengzi, he excelled in using coloring, power and brushing together to make his works unique, fresh and beautiful. He had published *Shuqi's Flowers and Birds Albums* and *Zhang Shuqi's Painting Albums*. This painting was created to celebrate a friend's birthday. The Crane stood for auspicious wishes. He painted in a clean and concise style with bright and gentle colors. The way he liked to use white power to mix with other colors was perfectly showed in the painting.

8. 近现代黄宾虹山水立轴

Huang Binhong's landscape vertical scroll in the modern times

　　该作品长142.5厘米，宽58.4厘米；纸本；浅绛山水画。

　　It is 142.5 cm in length, 58.4 cm in width; paper scroll; light-purple red landscape painting.

　　款识：昭平秋色戊辰七月，宾虹。

Inscription The Autumn Scenery in Zhaoping, the Seventh Month of the Year of Wuchen, Binhong.

商瞿祠堂共授经，三十年回首一灯青。风涛阅尽华容瘁，朝市茫更隐者名。几见微尘变沧海，不堪旧侣数晨星。金华山色独堪画，它日同攀可友亭。已巳六月。

It has been thirty years since we lectured the Confucian Classics together in the Memorial Hall of Shangqu with dim light. Having living through trials and hardships, the youthful looks fade away and even go to the morning market with an assumed name. Though the past years witnessed the the dramatic change from dusts to seas, the memory of staying with friends till counting morning is still unbearable to recall. Since the hills in Jinhua are so picturesque,why not climb to the Keyou Pavilion some day? June of the year of 1989.

钤印：黄质之印（白文）。

Stamp: Huang Zhi's Stamp (white).

黄宾虹（1865—1955年），原籍安徽省歙县，生于浙江金华，中国近现代国画家。他擅长山水画，兼作花鸟画；从事绘画史论和篆刻的研究、教学，并参与中国美术遗产的发掘、整理，以及相关图书的编纂、出版工作。新中国成立后，黄宾虹任中央美术学院华东分院教授、中国美术家协会华东分会副主席，被授予"中国人民优秀画家荣誉奖状"。该山水画作，层次深远，布局疏密有致，尺幅颇大，虽为作者中早期作品，但也足见其功力。

Huang Binhong (1865—1955), whose ancestral home is Shexian, Anhui, was born in Jinhua, Zhejiang. As an artist of traditional Chinese painting in modern China, he excelled in painting landscape as well as flowers and birds. He researched on and taught painting history and theories and seal cutting, and took charge of discovering, organizing, editing and publishing Chinese art heritage. After the founding of the People's Republic of China, Huang Binhong worked as professor in Central Academy of Fine Arts, East China Institute and vice president of China Artists Association East China Branch, and awarded with "China's Excellent Painter Honorary Credential". This landscape painting was featured with profound layers and well-spaced layout in a large size. It was his early work, but also revealed his outstanding skills.

9. 近现代蒋莲僧卅六洞天图

Jiang Lianseng's thirty six caves painting in the modern times

该作品长172厘米，宽40.7厘米；纸本；浅绛山水画。

It is 172 cm in length, 40.7 cm in width; paper scroll; light-purple red landscape painting.

款识：三十六洞天图，已巳夏至六月五日弟莲僧丌并记。

Inscription: Thirty Six Caves Painting Painted by Jiang Lianseng on June 5th.

钤印：莲道人（朱文），蒋瑞麒（白文）。

Stamp: Lian Dao Ren (red), Jiang Ruiqi (white).

蒋莲僧（1865—1943年），浙江金华人，少时与黄宾虹一起学画。清光绪年间秀才，生平致力于金石书画，其画艺精湛，出版《蒋莲僧画册》。金华地方绅士，1911年曾任金华府议长，后任教于浙江省立第七师范学校。三十六洞天为金华地方双龙名胜之首，此画为浅绛山水，色彩雅致、构图奇峻，为写生之作。

Jiang Lianseng (1865—1943) born in Jinhua, Zhejiang, learned painting with Huang Binhong when he was young and passed the imperial examination at the county level in the Qing Dynasty. He was a xiucai (one who passed the imperial examination at the county level), devoting to calligraphy and painting and was highly skilled in these fields. *Jiang Lianseng Painting Scroll* was published. As a local scholar in Jinhua, he served as speaker of Jinhua Office in 1911, later as a teacher in Zhejiang Provincial Seventh Normal School. Thirty-six caves is the most famous scenic spot in Jinhua Double Dragon National Park. This painting was light-purple red landscape one. Its elegant coloring and unique composition made it a real sketch from nature.

第二部分 金华各县市博物馆馆藏精品图鉴

Part 2
Collections of Jinhua Museums

第五章　兰溪市博物馆
Lanxi Museum

1. 三国半圆方枚神兽铜镜
Bronze mirror with semicircles and square patterns, the Three Kingdoms

该铜镜直径11.9厘米，钮径2.3厘米，缘厚0.4厘米。扁圆钮，钮座周饰一圈细微的月牙纹。内区周向式列坐高浮雕神人，或作独坐状，或作二人对坐晤谈状；间以龙虎鸾凤等禽兽。外区饰十三半圆纹，间以方枚，方枚内有"回、

子、师"等字。外区饰连珠、锯齿纹各一周，缘饰凸字形纹；铭文一圈，笔画多减省难以辨识。

The mirror is 11.9 cm in diameter, 2.3 cm in button diameter and 0.4 cm in rim thickness. It has a flat round button, with a circle of small crescent patterns around the button base. In the inner area, there sit high-relieved immortals around, some are sitting alone while some are talking, between whom, there decorated images of birds and beasts such as dragon, tiger, *luan* (a bird looks like phoenix) and phoenix. The outer area is decorated with thirteen semicircular patterns, with square patterns in the middle, being inscribed with Chinese characters of "回 (hui), 子 (zi), 师 (shi)". The outer area is designed with a circle decorated with patterns of a string of beads and a circle decorated with sawtooth patterns. There is a circle of inscriptions which are hard to distinguish because of the reduced strokes of characters.

2. 宋白釉瓷粉盒
White glazed porcelain compact, the Song Dynasty

该器口径10厘米，足径7厘米，通高5.7厘米。盒呈菊花形，圆唇、子母口、浅腹。盒内有3个小"碟"，间以四朵小莲蓬。通体施白，泛米黄色釉，釉面光润，胎质淡黄，造型别致。出土时，"碗"内应分别盛放粉、黛和胭脂的遗留物。

It is 10 cm in diameter, 7 cm in foot diameter and 5.7 cm in height. It takes a shape of a chrysanthemum, with round lips, loop mouth and shallow middle part. There are three small "die (small plates)" divided by four small lotuses. It is white entirely and smooth glazed, with light yellow carcass and unique shape. When unearthed, the "*wan* (small bowls)" should contain the remnants of powder, daisy and rouge respectively.

3. 北宋影青瓷注子
Misty blue porcelain pot (a wine vessel), the Northern Song Dynasty

该器通高16.2厘米，腹径15.3厘米，口径6.3厘米，底径9.1厘米。下凹形盖面，花蕾式盖钮。壶为敞口束颈瓜棱形腹，平底。通体施青白色釉，釉面莹润，形制精美，其式与陕西蓝田北宋吕氏家族墓M2（李大临墓）所出者近似。

It is 16.2 cm in over height, 15.3 cm in belly diameter, 6.3 cm in top diameter and 9.1 cm in bottom diameter, with a concave-shaped cover surface. The pot has an open mouth, a prism-shaped belly and a flat bottom. The whole body is painted with blueish white glaze whose surface is shiny. The shape is exquisite, being similar to the one unearthed in the M2 tomb (of Li Dalin) of the Lv family in the Northern Song Dynasty in Lantian, Shaanxi Province.

4. 北宋影青釉瓷碗
Misty white glazed porcelain bowl, the Northern Song Dynasty

该器口径9.8厘米，足径3厘米，高5厘米。1978年兰溪市灵洞乡回龙桥白塔坞出土。敞口，斜腹，圈足，施青白色釉，釉面莹润。

It is 9.8 cm in top diameter, 3 cm in foot diameter and 5 cm in height. In 1978, it was unearthed in Baitawu, Huilong Bridge, Lingdong Town, Lanxi City. It is featured with open mouth, oblique belly, circle feet, with shiny and smooth green white glaze.

5. 南宋双鱼纹金袋饰

Gold pocket accessory with patterns of double fish, the Southern Song Dynasty

该器长11厘米，宽3厘米。鱼袋是唐、宋时官员佩戴的证明身份之物。唐宋时期朝官与地方官吏，常用一种三寸长的鱼形饰物，作为彼此联络的凭证。鱼形饰物用金、银、铜等材料制成，上面刻有文字，分成两片，一片留在中央政府，另一片由地方官吏保存，如遇升迁等，即以此合符为证。金银饰也是鱼形。官员穿着公服时，则将鱼形金银饰系于带而垂于后，以明贵贱，并以此作为官吏出入殿门、城门的凭证。它起合契的作用，实际上就是古代虎符的变形。因为鱼目昼夜不闭，有"常备不懈"的寓意，所以被用作官员的装饰。

It is 11 cm in length and 3 cm in width. *Yudai* (a pocket accessory with fish patterns) was worn by officials in the Tang and Song Dynasties to prove their identity. In the Tang and Song Dynasties, court officials and local officials often used a three-inch fish-patterned accessory as a proof of communication with each other. The fish-shaped accessory is made of gold, silver, copper and other materials. The accessory with engraved characters can be divided into two pieces, one is kept in the central government, and the other is preserved by local officials. In case of promotion, this is the proof. The gold and silver ornaments are also fish-shaped. When wearing public uniforms, they are tied to the belt and hung behind to identify the noble and inferior, and to be used as a certificate for officials to come in and go out of the palace and city gates. It is functioned as a contract, another form of *hufu* (a tiger-shaped tally issued to generals as imperial authorization for troop deployment in ancient China). Since the fish eyes are not closed day and night, meaning "always being alert", they are used as decorations for officials.

宋代的官员服制，基本上沿袭唐代，宋代不用鱼符，只饰鱼形于袋上。凡有资格穿着紫、绯公服的官员，都可佩挂金、银装饰的鱼袋。《宋史·舆服志》云："鱼袋，其制自唐始，盖以为符契也。其始曰鱼符，左一右一，左者进内，右者随身，刻官姓名，出入合之。"在宋代，穿紫佩鱼是一种很高的荣誉。"赐紫"，是指官员的紫服是由朝廷直接颁赐的，并非其品级所能穿着。北宋赐鱼制度比较严格，不允许随意僭越。

The uniform system of officials in the Song Dynasty basically followed that of the Tang Dynasty. In the Song Dynasty, it was to use the fish-patterned pocket accessory not the fish-shaped tally. All officials who were qualified to wear purple and poppy official uniforms can wear gold or silver fish-patterned pocket accessory. *Song History · Yufuzhi* (*Records of Clothes in the History of the Song Dynasty*) said, "*yudai* had been regarded as a contract tally since the Tang Dynasty. It was originally named *yufu* (fish-shaped tally), divided into two parts. The left part was kept in the officials, while the right part was carried along. It was engraved with the official names and official positions. All can come in and go out when the left and right parts can be put together as a whole". In the Song Dynasty, it was a honor to wear the purple fish-patterned pocket accessory. The so-called "*cizi*" meant that he was directly awarded with the purple one by the court, which was actually not suitable for his rank. It was relatively strict to award the purple one in the Northern Song Dynasty, which could not be undertaken deliberately.

6. 南宋及斋长方形端砚
Jizhai rectangle duan inkstone, the Southern Song Dynasty

该砚长19.5厘米，宽11.5厘米，厚3.6厘米。石质淡紫色、湿润、细腻。此砚上窄下宽，呈"风"字样，底部刻有隶书"及斋"二字。此砚看上去朴素、大方，是宋代抄手砚的典型造型。"及斋"二字刀锋犀利、回锋刚劲、入石三分，结构平稳洒脱、刀法稳健，足见其功力。

It is 19.5 cm in length, 11.5 cm in width and 3.6 cm in thickness. It is lavender, smooth and delicate. It is narrow on the top and wide on the bottom, similarly forming a character of feng (wind). There engraved characters of "及斋 (*jizhai*)" at the bottom. The simple but generous inkstone was typical of *shouchao* (hand-written) inkstone in the Song Dynasty. The cutting skill of *jizhai* is sharp, strong and profound. The cutting way in the strokes of the two characters is stable and free, presenting a skilled technique.

7. 南宋棉毯

Cotton blanket, the Southern Song Dynasty

该棉毯长251厘米，宽116厘米，重1.58千克。棉毯细密厚实，以经纬线织成。两面拉毛均匀，呈淡黄色，黄中透白。棉毯上面用81枚开元通宝和北宋钱币排列成6个互相连接的菱形图案，其寓意不详。根据墓主人高氏是个女性推断，九九之积，可能表示"黄钟之数"，以音律的和谐来祈求子孙繁衍、家庭和睦。

It is 251 cm in length, 116 cm in width and 1.58 kg in weight. The cotton blanket is fine, thick and solid, woven with warp and weft threads. The two sides are evenly brushed, being light yellow or white in yellow. There are eighty-one Kaiyuan Tongbao and Northern-Song coins arranged in six interconnected diamond patterns, whose implication is still unknown. The tomb owner surnamed Gao was a female. The result of nine times nine might represent "number of huangzhong (a kind of counting using three times cardinal number)", presenting a harmonious tonality to pray for offspring's reproduction and peace.

8. 明宣德款铜香熏

Bronze censer during Xuande Period, the Ming Dynasty

该器长14.4厘米，宽11.45厘米，通高9.5厘米。子母口，直壁深腹，兽头足，凸底。盖顶中心为双龙卷云，四周及边缘为回字纹。底部铸有"大明宣德年制"方形标记。

It is 14.4 cm in length, 11.45 cm in width and 9.5 cm in height. It has a loop mouth, a straight and deep body, beast-patterned feet and a convex bottom. In the center of the top cover, there patterned with double dragons and cirrus clouds; while around the cover, there designed with "回"-shaped patterns. On the bottom, there casted a square mark of "Daming Xuande (Xuande Period of the Ming Dynasty)".

9. 明镂空雕梅枝犀角杯

Rhinoceros horns cup with design of pump branches, the Ming Dynasty

　　该器高9.2厘米。其杯口外撇，圆唇，器物呈不规则喇叭状，平底。外浮镂空雕梅花一枝，枝干苍虬；梅花十四朵、花蕾七朵。通体呈黄褐色，色泽莹润。雕刻刀法犀利、细腻流畅。其造型之美、构思之巧、雕镂之精，堪称精品。

　　It is 9.2 cm in height. The cup has a flared mouth, round lip, irregular trumpet-like shape and a flat bottom. There is one plum blossom carved out, whose branches and stems look like Cangqiu (a kind of dragon). There are fourteen plum blossoms and seven buds. It is yellowish brown, being shiny and smooth. The carving way is marvelous, delicate and smooth. The beauty of the shape, the ingenuity of the design and the precision of carving are the best.

　　犀角在古代与夜光璧、明月珠相提并论。道教文化中的八宝之一就有犀角。古人还有把犀角作为崇拜物的习俗，如青铜铸造、瓷器刻画等的犀角图案，他们认为犀牛可以辟邪、镇凶、保平安。还有一个更重要的原因，犀角本身就是一种名贵的药材。中医认为犀角具有清热解毒、凉血止血、镇惊等功效，明代李时珍的《本草纲目》中便有此记载。相传用犀角杯饮酒可以清热解毒，因此它便成为犀角器的主要器形。

Rhinoceros horns were on par with *yeguangbi* (a legendary luminous piece of jade with hole in center) and *mingyuezhu* (a legendary luminous pearl) in ancient times. The horn is one of the eight treasures of Taoist culture. Ancient people also regarded rhinoceros horns as the idol of the worship. For example, the designs of rhino horn were carved on bronzes and porcelains, which were believed to ward off evil spirits, suppress violence and bless with safety. There is a more important reason, rhino horn itself is a kind of precious medicinal material. Chinese medicine believes that rhino horn has the functions of clearing away heat and detoxifying, cooling blood and stopping bleeding, and suppressing convulsions, which was also mentioned in *Compendium of Materia Medica* written by Li Shizhen of the Ming Dynasty. According to the legend, drinking with rhino horn cup is good to clearing heat and removing toxicity, which promoted the production of horn cup.

10. 明永乐木刻版北藏经书
Classics of *Beizang*, Yongle Period of the Ming Dynasty

该作品长37厘米，宽13厘米，全书共计39册。

It is 37 cm in length, 13 cm in width, totaling 39 volumes.

《永乐北藏》又名《北藏》官版，是根据东汉以来流传中土的佛教经典加上唐玄奘从印度取来的经刻印的，由明成祖永乐八年（1410年）敕令雕印。官版藏经始刻于明成祖永乐十七年（1419年），于明英宗正统五年（1440年）竣工，参与者有道成、一如等。《永乐北藏》初刻本完成后，由于被藏在京城，一直作为官赐藏经，由朝廷印刷，下赐各地寺院。相较于其他佛经，它更具有官方性质和权威性。

Yongle Beizang is also named as *Beizang* officially, basing on the Buddhism scriptures of the Eastern Han Dynasty and the scriptures taken from India by Tang Xuanzang. It was carved by the imperial decree in the 8th year of Yongle Period of the Emperor Chengzu of the Ming Dynasty (1410). The official Tibetan scriptures were first inscribed in the 17th year of Yongle Period of the Emperor Chengzu of the Ming Dynasty (1419) and completed in the fifth year of Zhengtong Period of the Emperor Yingzong of the Ming Dynasty (1440). Daocheng, Yiru and others were engaged in it. After the completion of the first edition of *Yongle Beizang*, it was kept as an official Buddhist scriptures because it was kept in the capital. It was printed by the imperial court and given to various temples. Compared with other Buddhist scriptures, it is more official and authoritative.

明万历十二年（1584年），神宗因母后施印佛藏之愿，下敕雕造《永乐北藏》的《续入藏经》，并为之序。与初刻的《正藏》和《续藏》两项相加，至明万历十二年，《永乐北藏》已有677函（函号为"天"至"史"），收经1 651部、6 771卷。《本藏》共收经1 662部、6 924卷，分作693函，千字文函号自"天"至"塞"。《本藏》亦为折装本，但为了表现宫廷本的气魄，加大了字体与版心，每版25行，折为5个半页，每半页5行，每行17字，将字体改为秀丽的赵体。因为该版本专供颁赐各名山大寺之用，所以传世本较罕见。

In the twelfth year of Wanli Period of the Ming Dynasty (1584), the Emperor Shenzong issued the imperial decree of carving the part of *Xurucangjing* of *Yongle Beicang* to fulfill his mother's wish of printing Buddhist scriptures, and wrote a preface for it. Together with *Zhengcang* and *Xucang*, *Yongle Beicang* had already had 677 *han* (numbered from *tian* to *shi*), with 1,651 sections, totaling 6,771 volumes. *Bencang* had Buddhist scriptures of 1,662 sections, totaling 6,924 volumes, with 693 *han* numbered from *tian* to *sai*. This collection is also a folded version, with enlarged characters and type pages in order to present the spirit of the imperial version. There are 25 lines per page, being folded into five half pages with five lines per half page. There are 17 characters per line, and the character takes the Zhao type. Since this kind of version is rare to see, for it was bestowed to famous mountains and grand temples.

11. 新石器时代双孔石刀
Stone knife with double holes, the Neolithic Period

该器长9.5厘米，宽7.8厘米。

Length: 9.5 cm; width: 7.8 cm.

12. 战国米字纹硬陶罐
Pottery pot with *mi*-shaped patterns, the Warring States Period

该罐口径15.6厘米，腹径28.2厘米，底径14.9厘米，高23.2厘米。

Top rim diameter: 15.6 cm; belly diameter: 28.2 cm; bottom diameter: 14.9 cm; height: 23.2 cm.

13. 东汉青瓷双系罐
Celadon pot with double loops, the Eastern Han Dynasty

该罐口径10.4厘米，腹径20.6厘米，底径9.6厘米，高14厘米。

Top rim diameter: 10.4 cm; belly diameter: 20.6 cm; bottom diameter: 9.6 cm; height: 14 cm.

14. 东汉错金银凤纹青铜弩机

Bronze crossbow with patterns of golden and silver phoenix, the Eastern Han Dynasty

该器郭15.2厘米×3.3厘米×2.5厘米，望山8.6厘米×2.1厘米×0.9厘米。

Dimensions of Guo: 15.2 cm × 3.3 cm × 2.5 cm. Dimensions of Wangshan: 8.6 cm × 2.1 cm × 0.9 cm.

15. 西晋青瓷堆塑罐

Celadon pot with modeled figures, the Western Jin Dynasty

该罐口径13.7厘米，腹径25.4厘米，底径14.7厘米，高42.2厘米。

Top rim diameter: 13.7 cm; belly diameter: 25.4 cm; foot rim diameter: 14.7 cm; height: 42.2 cm.

16. 南朝婺州窑青瓷莲瓣纹碗

Celadon bowl with design of lotus petals of Wuzhou Kiln, the Southern Dynasty

该碗口径13.4厘米，足径6.1厘米，高7厘米。

Top rim diameter: 13.4 cm; foot rim diameter: 6.1 cm; height: 7 cm.

17. 唐婺州窑四系青瓷罐
Celadon pot with four loops of Wuzhou Kiln, the Tang Dynasty

该罐口径8.4厘米，腹径16.7厘米，底径7.4厘米，高14.7厘米。

Top rim diameter: 8.4 cm; belly diameter: 16.7 cm; bottom rim diameter: 7.4 cm; height: 14.7 cm.

18. **唐蝴蝶花鸟葵边铜镜**

Flower-shaped copper with patterns of butterfly, birds and flowers, the Tang Dynasty

镜径18.7厘米,缘厚0.5厘米,钮径2.3厘米。

Diameter: 18.7 cm; thickness: 0.5 cm; diameter of the button: 2.3 cm.

19. **宋仿剔漆如意云纹银盒(残)**

Imitated *tiqi* silver box with *ruyi* patterns (remains), the Song Dynasty

该盒残高4.9厘米，圆径15.4厘米。

Height of the remains: 4.9 cm; diameter: 15.4 cm.

1987年6月浙江省兰溪市灵洞乡费垅口村宋墓出土。

In June 1987, it was unearthed in a Song Tomb in Feilongkou Village, Lingdong Township, Lanxi City, Zhejiang Province.

20. 宋谷纹青玉瑗

Sapphire *yu'ai* (a kind of flat jade ring) with *gu*-patterns (a pattern of an upend "e"), the Song Dynasty

该器外径11.5厘米，内径6.6厘米，厚0.7厘米，外形基本完整。

Outer diameter: 11.5 cm; inner diameter: 6.6 cm; thickness: 0.7 cm; intact.

21. 北宋婺州窑青瓷执壶
Celadon pot with handle at side of Wuzhou Kiln, the Northern Song Dynasty

该壶口径8.6厘米，腹径17.4厘米，足径9.6厘米，高22.7厘米。

Top rim diameter: 8.6 cm; belly diameter: 17.4 cm; foot rim diameter: 9.6 cm; height: 22.7 cm.

22. 南宋金屈卮
Gold goblet, the Southern Song Dynasty

该器高5厘米，口径7.9厘米，足径3.6厘米。

Height: 5 cm; top rim diameter: 7.9 cm; foot rim: 3.6 cm.

23. 南宋"兰溪开国"铜印
Copper seal of "Lan Xi Kai Guo", the Southern Song Dynasty

该印长4.8厘米,宽4.8厘米,高3厘米。

Length: 4.8 cm; width: 4.8 cm; height: 3 cm.

24. 明铜尊
Bronze zun, the Ming Dynasty

该器通高15.1厘米,口径9.6厘米,底径4.4厘米,木制底座高3.6厘米。

Height: 15.1 cm; top rim diameter: 9.6 cm; bottom rim diameter: 4.4 cm; height of the wooden base: 3.6 cm.

25. 清德化窑白釉之暗款双铺首炉

White glazed stove with animal head applique of Dehua Kiln, the Qing Dynasty

该炉口径12.5厘米，腹径13.8厘米，足径10.5厘米，高7.8厘米。

Rim diameter: 12.5 cm; belly diameter: 13.8 cm; foot rim diameter: 10.5 cm; height: 7.8 cm.

第六章 义乌市博物馆
Yiwu Museum

1. 春秋青铜剑
Bronze sword, the Spring and Autumn Period

该剑长46厘米，宽3.5厘米。

Length: 46 cm; Width: 3.5 cm.

20世纪70年代义乌县佛堂镇杨宅村水坝工地出土。

It was unearthed from the dam construction site of Yangzhai Village, Fotang Town, Yiwu County in the 1970s.

剑身修长，剑锋尖锐，双刃犀利。剑身中线起脊，脊宽平，下端有一鸟纹图案，应为族徽或图腾象征。剑首为圆形，剑茎较短呈扁圆形，茎两边还有扁棱，以便手持或佩戴。整体来说，此剑制作精良，反映出当时精湛的青铜剑铸造技术与战争的频繁。

The sword has a slender body, a pointed blade, and two sharp edges. There was a ridge in the center line of the sword, which is wide and flat. At the bottom is a bird pattern which should be a symbol of the family emblem or totem. The head of the sword is round, and the stem is shorter and oblate, and there are flat edges on both sides of the stem for easy holding or wearing. On the whole, this sword is well-made, reflecting the exquisite bronze sword casting technology and the frequency of wars at that time.

2. 西汉原始瓷雕武士像兽首形耳玉璧绶带纹瓿

Primitive porcelain carving urn with a warrior portrait and beast head-shaped ears with jade ribbon patterns, the Western Han Dynasty

该器口径13厘米，底径18.3厘米，通高25.4厘米。

Top rim diameter: 13 cm; bottom rim diameter: 18.3 cm; height: 25.4 cm.

1962年义乌火车站基建工地出土。

It was unearthed from the infrastructure construction site of Yiwu Railway Station in 1962.

该器为短直口，平沿，斜广肩，扁圆腹，下腹内收，平底内凹。肩部两侧置对称双耳，耳面以圆圈纹和三角纹作地，并模印一个面目狰狞、一手举剑、

另一手执盾的披甲武士。前后腹部饰对称玉璧纹,璧面刻画圆圈纹(谷纹),璧上有半身人像,另有一绶带从上到下贯穿玉璧。肩腹部饰四组凹弦纹,其间饰有箭头纹和水波纹等。盖扁圆,缘内收作子口,顶部堆塑三个鸟形钮,并饰有水波纹等。该器施青黄色釉,釉不及下腹,大部分已剥落。

The urn has short and straight mouth, flat rim, oblique wide shoulders, flat round abdomen with retracted lower abdomen and concave flat bottom. Symmetrical ears are placed on both sides of the shoulders, which are grounded with circle patterns and triangle patterns, imprinted with a warrior who is sinister in appearance with a sword in one hand and a shield in the other. The front and back abdomen is decorated with symmetrical jade ribbon patterns, the surface of which is engraved with circular patterns (tadpole-like patterns). On the surface of the jade disc, there is a half-length portrait with a ribbon going through the jade disc from top to bottom. The shoulders and abdomen are decorated with four groups of concave string patterns, among which arrow patterns and water ripples are decorated. The cover is oblate, the edge is closed as a spigot, and the top is piled with three bird-shaped knobs decorated with water waves. It is painted with green-yellow glaze, which, however, cannot cover the lower abdomen, for most of the glaze has peeled off.

瓿作为青铜器主要流行于商代,一般用于盛放酒或水等液体,大多为圆体、大腹、带盖,有带耳与不带耳两种,亦有方形瓿。原始瓷瓿仿青铜器形制,是汉代比较常见的生活用具。本品原始瓷瓿的特点是纹饰少见,有身披铠甲、举剑持盾的武士,以及代表一定等级身份的玉璧、绶带等纹饰。因此,从这个的角度来看,这件文物应该是当时具有较高身份与社会地位的人士所用之器物。

Urns, as bronze wares, were mainly popular in the Shang Dynasty. They are generally used to contain liquids such as wine or water. Most of them are round with big abdomen and lid, while some of the urns are square. Some have ears, while some do not. The original porcelain carving urn was shaped like a bronze vessel, and it was a common household utensil in the Han Dynasty. The displayed porcelain urn is characterized by its rare ornamentation, which not only consists of a warrior wearing an armour and holding a sword and a shield, but also some jade discs that represent a certain level of identity. Therefore, from this point of view, this cultural relic should be an artifact used by people with higher social status at that time.

3. 东汉辟邪铜灯
Bixie bronze lamp, the Eastern Han Dynasty

该器通高9.4厘米。

Overall height: 9.4 cm.

2006年2月稠城街道倪大路村东汉砖室墓出土。

It was excavated from the brick chamber tomb of the Eastern Han Dynasty in Nidalu Village, Choucheng Sub-district, February 2006.

本品青铜辟邪前踞后蹲，昂首怒目，双眼突出，两耳竖起，口呈张开状，似欲扑击。唇下长须，四肢肥硕粗壮，背上正中和左前肢与背部交接处分铸出圆柱体和扁方体中空插筒各一，圆筒高于扁方筒。腹部中空，正上方圆管直通腹腔。全身饰龙鳞纹，纤毫毕现。

The displayed bronze Bixie, is groveling while squatting with head raised and glaring eyes protruding, ears erected, and mouth open, as if it were ready to pounce. It has long beards under the lips, sturdy limbs. At the center of the back and the junction of the left forelimb and the back were respectively cast a hollow cylinder and a flat cube. The cylinder is higher than the flat square tube. The abdomen is hollow, with a round tube directly reaching the abdominal cavity. The whole body is decorated with dragon scales, which is very delicate.

辟邪是古代传说中的神兽，似狮而有双翼，头生两角。这种翼兽始见于周代铜器，具有祛禳除恶的功能。汉代绘画、石刻、铜镜的辟邪纹饰屡见，但铜辟邪十分罕见。对同类或近似出土物的研究与对比发现，该青铜辟邪形器应为铜灯，其功用是古人用来照明的。其工艺精湛、造型灵动、细节刻画生动，为一件难得的青铜珍品。

Bixie is a divine beast in ancient legends, resembling a lion with wings and two horns. This kind of winged beast was first seen on the bronze ware of the Zhou Dynasty, and it has the function of eliminating scorpion and evil. It was common in the paintings, stone carvings, and bronze mirror patterns of the Han Dynasty but copper Bixie was very rare. Through the comparative research of kindred or similar unearthed objects, the displayed bronze evil-shielding device should be a copper lamp, whose function was used by ancients for lighting. Its exquisite craftsmanship, smart shape and vivid details make it a rare bronze treasure.

4. 东汉鎏金五乳神兽镜

Gilt bronze mirror with divine beasts and five nails, the Eastern Han Dynasty

该镜直径14厘米，缘厚0.7厘米。

Diameter: 14 cm; rim thickness: 0.7 cm.

义乌县徐村乡出土。

It was unearthed at Xucun Village, Yiwu County.

该镜为半圆形钮，重圈钮座。内区以五乳间隔五区，主纹为青龙、朱雀、白虎、玄武、羽人骑神兽。主纹外圈饰"尚方作镜真大巧，上有仙人不知老，渴饮玉泉饥食（枣）"20个字隶书铭文。除外区之外，该镜镜背内区采用的是鎏金工艺。鎏金工艺是我国古代器物装饰的一种特殊工艺，是将金和水银合成金汞剂，涂在铜器表面，然后加热使水银蒸发，而金则附着于器表不脱落。鎏金工艺作为春秋战国时期青铜器铸造工艺的延伸，至汉代已较发达。而相较于鎏金铜器，鎏金铜镜的发现数量极少。

It has a semi-circular knob against a loopy knob seat. The inner area is separated into five small areas by five nails. The main patterns are represented by the Azure Dragon, the Vermilion Bird, the White Tiger, the Black Tortoise, and the Feather Man who is riding the mythical creature. The outer ring of the main pattern is decorated with a 20-character inscription in the official script "尚方作镜真大巧，上有仙人不知老，渴饮玉泉饥食（枣）". Except the outside area, all of the inner areas of the back of the mirror are made by gilding technology. The gilding process is a special craft for decoration of ancient utensils in China. It is to synthesize gold and mercury into a gold amalgam and paint it on the surface of the copperware before the mercury is heated to evaporation, while the gold still adheres to the surface of the vessel without falling off. As an extension of the bronze casting process during the Spring and Autumn Period and Warring States Period, the gilt craft had been more developed in the Han Dynasty. Compared with gilt bronzes, the discovery of gilt bronze mirrors seems to be extremely rare.

5. 东晋铜六面印

Copper hexahedron seal, the Eastern Jin Dynasty

该印高3厘米，底边长1.8厘米。

Height: 3 cm; length: 1.8 cm.

1994年9月义乌市义亭镇畈田朱村朱福田上交。

It was handed in by Zhu Futian, Zhu Village, Fantian, Yiting Town, Yiwu City, September 1994.

该印为正方形印面，方钮。印共有六面，印面文字均为细线白文小篆体。钮顶部印文为"白记"，座底部印文为"朱赟"，座侧面印文依次为"朱少素""朱赟白事""臣赟""朱赟白牋"。除二面有边栏外，其余均无边栏。六面印是魏晋六朝时期盛行的一种印章款式。"臣""白事""白牋"等是当时私印的专用语。从目前的考古出土材料来看，六面印只见于东晋时期，其他时期没有出土。其造型比较规范，呈现"凸"字形，尺寸大小都差不多，六个面都有印文，印文一般为墓主人的名和字。现在的研究认为，"六面印"应为私印，一印而具有多面印文，就是一印多用途，印主一般应是当时有一定身份和地位的官宦士族。

With square seal surfaces and a square knob, the seal has six sides, all of which are engraved with light-face characters of Bai nationality in small seal style. The seal on the top of the button is "白记 (Baiji)", the seal on the bottom of the base is "朱赟 (Zhu Yun)", and the seals on the four sides of the base are "Zhu Shaosu", "Zhu Yun Baishi", "Chen Yun", and "Zhu Yun Baijian". With sidebars on only two sides, the rest have no sidebars. Six-side seal was a popular seal style during the Wei, Jin Period and Six Dynasties. "Chen" "Bai Shi" "Bai Jian", etc. were the special terms of private seals at that time. Judging from the current unearthed archaeological materials, the six-side seal was only seen in the Eastern Jin Dynasty, which has never been unearthed in other periods yet. The shape is relatively standardized, all showing a "A" shape (more resembling a Chinese character "凸"), with similar size and different seals of each side, generally engraved with the family name and the given name of the owner of the tomb. Researchers now believe that the six-side seal should be a private seal, owing to the fact that there are multiple seals printed on one seal, which means that one seal was made into multiple uses. The seal owner should probably be a member of the official family with a high social status at that time.

6. 唐三彩鸳鸯纹釉陶枕

Tri-colored ceramic pillow glazed with mandarin duck pattern, the Tang Dynasty

该枕长12.5厘米，宽10.1厘米，高5.5厘米。

Length: 12.5 cm; width: 10.1 cm; height: 5.5 cm.

1978年3月义乌县田心公社田心四村金鸡笼山出土。

It was unearthed from Jinjilong Mountain, Tianxin 4th Village, Tianxin Commune, Yiwu County in March 1978.

该陶枕为长方形，灰白胎；釉以绿、黄、蓝三色为主，多处已剥落。枕面微内凹，刻画出内外两个长方形边框；内框刻画交颈鸳鸯戏莲纹，活灵活现，富有浪漫气息和生活情趣。除枕面外，其余各面均为素面。特别值得一提的是，这是一件挂蓝彩的三彩器，其上施的蓝釉是进口的钴料，这种钴料大多通过丝绸之路经国外贸易交换而来。俗话说："三彩挂蓝，价值连城"，足见其珍罕程度。总体来看，此枕形制规整、精致小巧，保存基本完整，特别是义乌本地出土，这对研究当时南北方之间的贸易往来具有重要的实证价值。

It is rectangular with gray-white body. The glaze is mainly green, yellow and blue, many parts of which have peeled off. The pillow surface is slightly concave where two rectangle frames carved on the inside and outside. On the inner frame areas is carved the pattern of the cross-necked mandarin duck playing lotus, which is vivid and full of romance and life interests. Except the pillow surface, all other surfaces are plain. It is particularly noteworthy that this is a thi-colored ware dotted with blue color. The blue glaze painted on it is made from imported cobalt, most of which is exchanged from foreign trade through the Silk Road. The old saying "three colors with blue are priceless" exactly shows its rarity. On the whole, this pillow-shaped system is regular, exquisite and compact, and remain mostly intact, especially unearthed locally in Yiwu, which has important empirical value for studying the trade exchanges between North and South at that time.

7. 五代越窑青瓷带盖执壶

Celadon ewer with handle at side made in Yue kiln, the Five Dynasties

该壶口径4.6厘米，底径8.1厘米，通高20.1厘米。

Top rim diameter: 4.6 cm, Bottom rim diameter: 8.1 cm, Height: 20.1 cm.

1977年义乌县廿三里公社王店村出土。

It was unearthed in Wangdian Village, Niansanli Commune, Yiwu County in 1977.

该壶为直口，长颈，丰肩，圆鼓腹，矮圈足外撇。肩部一侧有微曲长流，稍低于子口，另一侧置一双泥条曲柄，柄端高于口沿。盖为母口，盖顶饰弦纹三道，宝珠钮，盖壁有两个圆形穿孔用以穿系。此壶为灰白胎，胎质细密，施青绿色釉。壶底和盖内顶部有长条形泥点支烧痕。

It has a straight mouth, long neck, and broad shoulders, as well as round abdomen with short ringed feet outwards. There is a slightly curved long spigot on one side of the shoulder, slightly lower than the outer spout, and a pair of clay strips of cranks placed on the other side, the handle end of which is higher than the mouth edge. Under the lid is the main spout and the top of the lid is decorated with three strings of patterns, a pearl knob. On the lid wall are two circular perforations, which are used for threading. The porcelain body is gray-white with delicate texture painted with green glaze. There are long strips of clay dots, calcinating marks, on the bottom and the top of the lid.

执壶又称注子，是一种盛酒器。执壶出现于唐代中期，到了晚期，壶的种类增多，有喇叭口壶、直口壶、侈口壶、长颈壶、短颈壶、筒颈壶等。腹多呈瓜棱形，流呈多棱，把为扁带状，釉色以青黄色居多。其造型基本上朝着两种形式演变：一种为颈部渐高，腹渐瘦长，作瓜棱形，流变长；另一种为颈部渐高，腹渐圆，流变长，式样更加优美。此件执壶属于五代越窑制品，其造型特点是腹部浑圆，流呈圆形弧曲。从整体上看，此器器形典雅、饱满中正、线条优美，是一件难得的越窑佳品。

The ewer, also known as "*Zhuzi*" (an ancient Chinese drinking vessel), is a wine container. The ewer appeared in the middle of the Tang Dynasty. In the late period, the types of pots increased, ranging from flared pots, straight pots, wide flared mouth pots, long-necked pots and short-necked pots, to tube-necked pots. The abdomens mostly have melon ridges, the spout is multi-ridged, the handle is flat ribbon shaped, and the glaze is mostly blue and yellow. The figure basically evolves in two forms: one type has a gradually rising neck while the abdomen becomes thinner and longer like a melon with a longer spigot; the other type also has a gradually higher neck but the abdomen becomes rounder, when the flow also becomes longer, which is more beautiful in style. This ewer is one of Yue kiln products of the Five Dynasties period characterized by a round abdomen and a circular spout. On the whole, this vessel is elegant in shape, plump and upright with fine lines, which represents a treasure of Yue kiln products.

8. 北宋铜观音菩萨立像
Copper statue of standing Buddha, the Northern Song Dynasty

该立像通高26厘米。

Overall height: 26 cm.

1984年3月义乌县塘李乡景德寺遗址窖藏出土。

It was unearthed from the cellar of the Jingde Temple site in Tangli Township, Yiwu County in March 1984.

菩萨像顶束发髻，额发为螺旋式，面容丰腴，眉清目秀。菩萨像双唇微闭，面带微笑，双耳垂肩，双手合于腹部，施禅定印。其上身披通肩长袖衣；下身着长裙，衣褶线条流畅；跣足立于仰覆莲座上。像后有头光和背光，头光外层铸火焰纹，内层呈椭圆形，并有莲瓣纹；背光为火焰纹，下部与足齐平。该铜观音菩萨立像保存基本完整，出土于佛寺遗址窖藏，对于研究宋代义乌地区的佛教信仰具有重要的历史和文物价值。

With a hairpin on the head as well as a spiral forelock, the figure of Bodhisattva shows a plump face, bright eyes and graceful eyebrows. The lips are slightly closed with a smile. The ears fall over the shoulders with palms folded on the abdomen as mudra of meditation. The upper body is covered with a shoulder-covering long-sleeved shirt, while on the lower body, it wears a long skirt with smooth pleated lines, sitting on the lotus throne barefoot. There is a headlight and a backlight behind the image. The outer layer of headlight is cast with flame patterns, and the inner layer is oval with lotus petal patterns. The backlight is a flame pattern, the lower part of which is flush with the feet. The bronze statue of Guanyin Bodhisattva remains mostly intact. It was unearthed from the cellar of Buddhist temple sites and of significant historical and cultural value for the study of Buddhist beliefs in Yiwu during the Song Dynasty.

9. 北宋錾刻人物故事银花片
Silver slices with carved figures, the Northern Song Dynasty

该器长32.4厘米，高24厘米。

Length: 32.4 cm; Height: 24 cm.

1986年12月义乌县柳青乡游览亭村窖藏出土。

It was unearthed from the cellar in Youlanting Village, Liuqing Township, Yiwu County, December 1986.

该银花片为长方形，倭角。其纹饰有内外两区组成：外区上下分别饰缠枝番莲纹，左右饰缠枝菊瓣纹，四角饰卷草纹，并衬以珍珠地；内区錾刻两个人物，其中一位老者拄杖立于古松下，另一人策步向老者，左手指向跪于地上觅食的四只羊。画面的故事源自金华地区流传甚广的神话故事"叱石成羊"。相传汉时，牧童黄初平牧羊时偶遇道士，随之修道，后其兄寻至，初平以仙术将白石化为羊群。典出晋代葛洪的《神仙传·卷二》。后来，"叱石成羊"被作为成语广为流传，其原意是得道成仙、法术高妙，喻指神奇的事情。

It is rectangular with multiple angles. The decoration is composed of inner and outer areas: the upper and lower parts of the outer area are respectively decorated with tangled lotus pattern pattern, the left and right parts chrysanthemum petals pattern and the four corners curly grass patterns against pearls. Two figures are engraved in the inner area. One is an old man who is standing under the ancient pine with a stick ,while the other is a man who is walking towards the old man with his left hand pointing to four sheep kneeling on the ground and looking for food. The story shown in the picture originates from the myth of turning the stone into a sheep, which is widely spread in Jinhua. The *Legend of Gods (Volume Two)* written by Ge Hong in the Jin Dynasty recorded that Huang Chuping, a shepherd boy in the Han Dynasty, encountered a Taoist priest while he was shepherding sheep and followed him for the Taoism. Later, his brother found him, only to see that Chuping turned white stones into a flock of sheep by using mantra. Later, the idiom — "Chi Shi Cheng Yang" (to turn a stone into a sheep) has been widely circulated as an idiom. The original meaning of this idiom refers to the fact that one becomes an immortal with magical skills, while the metaphorical meaning refers to something magical.

10. 北宋青瓷蕉叶纹四系盖罐
Celadon covered jar with focal leaf patterns, the Northern Song Dynasty

该罐口径9.3厘米,底径9.8厘米,通高18.6厘米。

Top rim diameter: 9.3 cm; bottom rim diameter: 9.8 cm; height: 18.6 cm.

1990年5月义乌稠城镇仓后路建筑工地出土。

It was unearthed from the construction site of Canghou Road in Choucheng Town, Yiwu City in May 1990.

该罐为子母口微敞,圆唇,短直颈,鼓腹,圈足外撇。颈肩部有双泥条和单泥条系各一对,四系相互间隔对称。腹部刻有仰蕉叶纹,分上、中、下三层,每层九瓣。盖为圆形,尚刻覆蕉叶纹,钮残缺。此盖罐为灰白胎,细致坚实。通体施青绿色釉,釉薄而光亮。圈足底部留有垫圈支烧痕。此盖罐整器式样规整、制作精细,施釉虽薄,却光洁莹澈、涵青蕴翠,纹饰风格纤细淡雅、精美流畅,是一件工艺水准极高的宋代青瓷作品。

With spout and spigot slightly open, the celadon jar has round lips, short straight neck, bulging belly and curling outward feet. There are a pair of double mud bars and a single mud bar on the neck and shoulders, and the four groups are spaced symmetrically. The abdomen is engraved with the pattern of upside down banana leaves, divided into upper, middle and lower layers, each with nine petals. The lid is round, which is still engraved with a banana leaf pattern and the knob is incomplete. Other physical characteristics include an ash-grey body, which is delicate and firm, and blueish green glaze, whose surface is shiny as well as burning circle marks on the bottom of the ring foot. This lidded porcelain has a neat style and delicate production. Although the glaze is thin, it looks crystal clear and verdant green. The style of emblazonry is slender and elegant, exquisite and smooth, making it hailed as a piece of the celadon work of Song Dynasty with extremely high craftsmanship.

11. 北宋金龙
Gold dragon, the Northern Song Dynasty

该器长15.5厘米，重6.8克。

Length: 15.5 cm; Weight: 6.8 g.

1984年3月义乌县塘李乡景德寺遗址窖藏出土。

It was unearthed from the cellar of the Jingde Temple in Tangli Town, Yiwu City in March 1984.

该金龙为鳄鱼形头，双角分叉似鹿角，圆眼，猪嘴，张口状，舌呈如意头形，舌上含一宝珠。颈细长，有鬣毛卷向颈部，由颈至腹部逐渐变粗，近上腹部有"许旦"刻款。四肢粗壮有力，四爪弯曲似鹰爪，虎尾，尾端上翘。整条龙采用了单面錾刻工艺，龙身饰鱼鳞纹，错落有致。细看金龙，其风格洗练精纯，气韵生动，细节逼真写实。1995年5月5日，北宋金龙被定为国家一级文物，成为义乌市博物馆的镇馆之宝。

It has a crocodile-shaped head with double horns bifurcated like antlers, round eyes and an open snout with a pearl on the top of its S-shaped tongue. It also has a long and thin neck, to which the curly hair extends.From the neck to the abdomen, the body gradually becomes thicker and near the upper abdomen is engraved the inscription "Xu Dan (许旦)". With sturdily built limbs, the four claws curve like eagle claws when the tiger-like tail is upturned. The whole dragon applies a single-sided gilt carving technology, and the dragon body is decorated with fish scales in a patchwork pattern. Looking closely at the gold dragon, it is refined and pure in style, vivid with charm and realistic in details. The gold dragon of the Northern Song Dynasty was designated as a national first-class cultural relic and became the treasure of the Yiwu Museum on May 5, 1995.

12. 北宋錾刻人物故事纹鎏金银台盏

Flower-shaped gilt silver bowl carved with figures, the Northern Song Dynasty

盏（上）：口径11.6厘米，底径4.4厘米，高3.8厘米；托（下）：底径17.5厘米，高5.5厘米。

Cup (up): top rim diameter: 11.6 cm; bottom rim diameter: 4.4 cm; height: 3.8 cm. Holder (down): bottom diameter: 17.5 cm; height: 5.5 cm.

1986年12月义乌县柳青乡游览亭村窖藏出土。

It was unearthed from the cellar in Youlanting Village, Liuqing Township, Yiwu County, December 1986.

盏：花口外撇，圆唇，弧腹斜收，圈足外撇。口沿内侧錾刻一周宽为0.65厘米的鎏金珍珠地缠枝卷草纹带。内底心有直径约为3.7厘米的圆形錾刻鎏金高士饮酒图案。

Cup: the flower-shaped mouth is rolled outwards, the lips are rounded, the arc belly is closed obliquely. The circle of the foot is rolled outward. The inner side of the mouth is engraved with a 0.65 cm wide gilt-and-pearl grounded curling grass pattern. There is designed with a 3.7 cm-in-width round gilded pattern of a drinking scholar.

托：花口，圆唇内卷，喇叭形圈足。盘口内缘錾刻一周缠枝番莲纹。内托凸起于盘面。盏托较浅，圆形盏座。

Holder: it is flower-shaped. The round lip curls inward, with a flared ring-shaped foot. The inner rim of the mouth is engraved with a tangled lotus pattern. The inner part of the holder is higher than the surface while holder is shallow and round.

台盏，是指有托的杯子。它是酒盏与酒台子的合称，是酒器中的一种固定组合。其中，酒台子是承托酒盏之盘，盘心凸起加一倒扣的小盏以为承台，因此而得名。台盏是一种高级酒具，不能与普通的托盏、盏托混为一谈。《辽史·礼志三》有重要仪式中贵族"执台盏进酒"的记载："宋使祭奠吊慰仪……大使近前跪，捧台琖，进奠酒三，教坊奏乐，退，再拜。"《元史·舆服志》则将台盏定为区别官员官阶的器皿之一，对其使用规格作了限制。由此可见，此类台盏在古代社会生活和礼仪活动中具有重要地位与作用。

Taizhan, is a cup with holder. It is the collective name of the wine cup and the holder, and it is a fixed combination among wine vessels. Among them, the holder is to support the wine cup. It is combined by placing the upside-down small cup on the raised holder. *Taizhan* is a high-end wine set, which should not be confused with ordinary holders. *Lizhisan of Liao History* recorded the important ceremony of the nobles holding *taizhan* for wine, saying that the Song ambassador paid a memorial service... the ambassador kneeled down in front, holding *taizhan* with sacrifice wine. When the music rang, the ambassador backed up and bowed again. *Yufu zhi of Yuan History* designated *taizhan* as one of the vessels for distinguishing the ranks of officials and restricted its specifications. It can be seen that this type of *taizhan* played an important role in ancient social life and ritual activities.

13. 元龙泉青瓷鱼形砚滴
Longquan celadon fish-shaped *yandi* (water receptacle), the Yuan Dynasty

该砚滴长12.2厘米，高6.8厘米。灰白胎，较致密。整体造型呈一尾昂头翘尾的鲤鱼，鱼嘴为出水孔，背部有一注水小孔。鱼身暗刻鳞片错落有致，左右胸鳍、腹鳍外展作支撑的四足，背鳍与尾鳍之间呈凹状。通体施青釉，釉色青莹、滋润、肥厚。足底露胎垫烧，呈淡火石红色。砚滴为古时文房用具，也称水滴、水注，为滴水入砚、研磨墨汁之用。宋元时期，瓷质砚滴十分流行，品种也很丰富，其中又以龙泉窑烧造的砚滴的造型最为新颖别致，此件鱼形砚滴即其中一例。仿动物造型历来为砚滴的一大传统，而鱼跃龙门又是一个非常吉祥的隐喻，因此，鱼形砚滴是社会文化绝佳的载体。本品摹形生动，釉水纯正，尺寸较一般砚滴大。从其造型看，似还可作笔搁之用，可谓龙泉青瓷文化的一件代表作。

It is 12.2 cm in length and 6.8 cm in width. It is grey and dense. It takes a shape of carp with head and tail up in the air. Its mouth is a water outlet, and its back has a small hole for water injection. The fish body is darkly carved with scales, well-proportioned. The left and right pectoral and pelvic fins are abducted as the four feet for support. There is a concave between the back fin and the tail fin. It is celadon glazed completely. The glaze is lustrous, transparent, smooth and rich. The bottom of the foot is fired, presenting light flint red. *Yandi*, an ancient writing tool, is also called *shuidi* (water drip) or *shuizhu* (water spout), for it was used to drip water into the inkstone to grind ink. During the Song and Yuan Dynasties, the porcelain *yandi* was very popular, with a rich variety. Among them, *yandi* made in Longquan kiln was the most novel and unique, including this fish-shaped *yandi*. It has always been a tradition of *yandi* taking the shape of animals. Since a fish leaping over the dragon gate (referring to a scholar has passed through a competitive examination) is a very auspicious metaphor, the fish-shaped *yandi* is an excellent carrier of social culture. This *yandi* is vivid, with pure glaze, larger than the ordinary ones. From its shape, it seems that it can also be used as an ink brush holder. It can be described as a representative of Longquan celadon culture.

14. 元龙泉青瓷玉壶春瓶
Celadon vase made in Longquan, the Yuan Dynasty

该瓶口径7.5厘米，底径7.8厘米，高27.3厘米。

Top rim diameter: 7.5 cm; foot rim diameter: 7.8 cm; height: 27.3 cm.

1985年9月义乌县工人路窖藏出土。

It was unearthed from the cellar of Gongren Road, Yiwu Country in September 1985.

该瓶为喇叭形口，口沿外翻，圆唇，细长颈，溜肩，圆垂腹，圈足，鸡心底。灰白胎，胎质坚密。通体施粉青釉，釉色青翠匀净，釉面滋润肥厚。外观柔和淡雅，如冰似玉。底足满釉，圈足露胎处呈现火石红。该器出自元代龙泉窑瓷器窖藏，整体保存状态良好，造型优美，沉稳典雅，是一件难得的元代龙泉窑精品。

It takes a shape of a trumpet, with flared mouth, round lip, slender neck, sloping shoulder, round sagging belly, ringed foot and heart-shaped bottom. It is evenly glazed with lavender grey, pure and fresh. The glaze is lustrous, smooth and rich. It is soft and elegant outside, resembling ice and jade. The bottom foot is glazed fully, with the flint red rim of the exposed foot. This ware came from the Longquan kiln porcelain cellar of the Yuan Dynasty. It is preserved in good condition, beautiful, tasteful and elegant. It is a rarely fine product of Longquan kiln in the Yuan Dynasty.

15. 明崇祯十三年（1640年）《义乌县志》

Yi Wu Xian Zhi (Log of the Yiwu County), the thirteenth year of Chongzhen of the Ming Dynasty, 1640

该作品版框尺寸为29.6厘米×20.7厘米，全6册，20卷。2002年4月山东省安丘县博物馆调拨。

Dimensions: 29.6 cm×20.7 cm, 6 books, 20 volumes. It was allocated by Anqiu County Museum, Shandong Province in April 2002.

全书共6册、20卷，由当时义乌县令熊人霖主修而成。半页7~9行，每行13~20字不等。全书分为《县图》《方舆》《经制》《物土》《时务》《勇为》《人物》《杂述》等篇，体例严谨、考订详富，对研究古代义乌的经济、地理、人文等具有重要的史料价值。崇祯十三年《义乌县志》原由山东省安丘县博物馆收藏，2002年4月12日经国家文物局批准，调拨给浙江省义乌市博物馆收藏。

There were a total of 6 books with 20 volumes, composed by Xiong Renlin, the magistrate of Yiwu County at that time. There are 7 to 9 lines each half page and about 13 to 20 characters each line. It has chapters of "Xiantu" "Fangyu" "Jingzhi" "Wutu" "Shiwu" "Yongwei" "Renwu" and "Zashu". It has strict rules in writing and prudential examining, presenting an important historical value for a research on the economy, geography, and humanities of ancient Yiwu. *Yi Wu Xian Zhi* (Log of the Yiwu Country) of the thirteenth year of Chongzhen of the Ming Dynasty was originally collected by the Anqiu County Museum in Shandong Province, and was allocated to the Yiwu City Museum in Zhejiang Province on April 12, 2002 with the approval of the National Cultural Heritage Administration.

16. 明金丝髢髻

The spun gold hairnet, the Ming Dynasty

该器口径10.5厘米，高6.5厘米，重41.6克。

Rim diameter: 10.5 cm; height: 6.5 cm; weight: 41.6 g.

1996年12月义乌市青口乡官塘塍村，嘉靖三十七年吴鹤山之妻金氏墓出土。

It was excavated from the tomb (set up in the 37th year during the reign of Jiajing in the

Ming Dynasty) of Wu Heshan's wife Jin in Guantangcheng Village, Qingkou Town, Yiwu City in December, 1996.

该鬏髻由圈、檐、盖三部分组成。它由极细金丝编结成网状，以三根较粗金丝穿连，左右两侧有外圆内方的钱纹图案各三个。全器薄如蝉翼，工艺精湛。

The hairnet consists of a ring, a brim and a cap altogether three parts. It is made of extremely fine golden wires which are woven into a net connected by three relatively thick golden wires. On each side are three patterns of coin that is the round outside and square inside. Due to exquisite craftsmanship, the entire ware is as thin as the cicada's wing.

鬏髻是明代妇女的主要发式，一般用马尾、头发或金银丝等材料编成，呈中空的网状圆锥体。妇女使用时将其扣在头顶，罩住由真发结成的发髻。鬏髻只是用来罩住顶发，而非整个头部，因此尺寸一般都不大，底部口宽仅十几厘米，又被称为"发鼓"。遇有重要的场合，鬏髻上要插戴包括分心、挑心、花钿和金银簪等在内的成套首饰，称为"头面"。

The hairnet is women's main hairstyle in the Ming Dynasty. It is usually made of horsetails, hairs or golden and silver wires, and shaped as a hollow cone net. When using, women wear it on the head to cover the bun made by the real hair. Because the hairnet, also known as the hair drum, only covers the top hair, it is usually not large-sized. The width of the bottom mouth is only over 10 cm. On important occasions, women should wear a whole set of jewelries, known as head ornaments, on the hairnet, including the splitting center hairpin, the lifting center hairpin, floral accessories and gold or silver hairpins.

明代出嫁的妇女一般都要戴鬏髻，因此它是女性已婚身份的标志。由于身份、家境的差异，妇女佩戴的鬏髻材质也各不相同，比较常见的有三种，即头发鬏髻、银丝鬏髻、金丝鬏髻。

Married women in the Ming Dynasty usually wear hairnets, and hence it is a sign of the married status. Because of the difference in identity and family background, the hairnets wore by women are also made of different materials. Three types are relatively common, hair hairnets, spun silver hairnets and spun gold hairnets.

金丝鬏髻是鬏髻中最贵重的一种，通常做成扁圆的冠状，因此又称作"金冠""金丝梁冠儿"。佩戴金冠是官宦人家的正室夫人才能享受的特权，是尊贵地位的象征。迄今为止，我国出土的金丝鬏髻数量很少，最具有代表性的就是吴鹤山之妻金氏墓出土的金丝鬏髻。

The spun gold hairnet, usually made into a flat and round coronary shape, is the most valuable one among hairnets, so it is also called "golden crown" or "spun gold crown". The gold hairnet is a symbol of the exalted status and the privilege enjoyed by wives in the official families. Up to now, the number of the unearthed spun gold hairnets is quite few and the most representative is the one excavated from the tomb of Wu Heshan's wife Jin.

17. 清奉天诰命圣旨箱

The imperial edict box inscribed with "following God's will and royal order", the Qing Dynasty

该箱长43厘米，宽35.5厘米，高43.5厘米。

Length: 43 cm; width: 35.5 cm; height: 43.5 cm.

2000年5月毛店镇朱店村征集。

It was collected from Zhudian Village, Maodian Town in May, 2000.

该箱为樟木质，长方形，缺盖。它采用浮雕技法，中部阳刻楷书"奉天诰命"；两侧刻五爪立龙，龙尾回旋相接；上刻双龙戏珠，下刻水波纹，间以祥云点缀；其余四面亦刻龙纹、祥云、海水纹。箱体正面的"奉天诰命"四字代表皇室的尊严至高无上，下部的海水江崖表示一统天下、江山永固。在明清之际，五品以上官员，如果功绩超群都有机会得到皇帝的封赠命令，即诰命。据《清会典》记载，针对官员本身的诰命叫诰授（即"奉天诰命"）；针对官员之妻的叫诰封（即"凤冠诰命"）。本件奉天诰命箱保存基本完整，工艺精湛。据考证，此箱应为义乌名人朱一新家旧物，因此具有极高的历史、文化与艺术价值。

The box is made of camphorwood, rectangular and missing a lid. The technique of embossing is adopted and the characters in regular script, "following God's will and royal order", are inscribed convexly. On two sides are five-clawed dragons with convoluting tails connected with each other. On the upside are engraved two dragons frolicking with a pearl and on the downside are the patterns of waves, with auspicious clouds interspersed in between. On the other four sides are also engraved patterns of dragons, auspicious clouds and waves. The four characters "following God's will and royal order" on the facade represent the supreme imperial dignity, and the seawater and cliff on the downside represent the unity of the whole country and the everlasting reign. In the Ming and Qing Dynasties, if with preeminent feats, the official above the fifth rank would receive the appointment and bestowal order, i.e. the imperial order. According to *The Code of the Qing Dynasty*, to officials, royal order is royal bestowal (following the God's will and royal order); to officials' wives, it is called royal appointment (the royal order of phoenix coronet). This imperial order box is completely preserved and expertly crafted. According to the textual research, it is the antique from the family of a Yiwu celebrity Zhu Yixin, and therefore is equipped with quite high historical, cultural and artistic values.

18. 清青白玉瑞兽衔芝摆件

Bluish-white jade decoration with the shape of an auspicious beast holding a Ganoderma in the mouth, the Qing Dynasty

该摆件长14厘米，高7.4厘米。

Length: 14 cm; height: 7.4 cm.

该器玉质温润，带黄褐皮，光泽度较高。兽首额部宽平，嘴衔一灵芝，前肢蹲伏，后腿作蹬状，扁平卷毛尾；全身肌肉丰满，毛发线条流畅。整体来看，这件玉雕作品用料足，采用圆雕、透雕等工艺，局部巧雕，雕工精湛，形神皆备，颇为有趣，为清代中期玉雕作品中的一件精品。

The material of jade is gentle with yellowish-brown crust and has high gloss. The forehead on the head of the beast is broad and flat. With a ganoderma in its mouth, the beast crouches with its forelegs and stamps with its hindlegs. It has a flat curly tail, plumb full-body muscle and a sleek fur. As a whole, this jade carving uses sufficient materials, adopts methods such as round engraving and piercing engraving. Some parts are delicately engraved and the crafts are exquisite, achieving unity in form and spirit and making it excellently intriguing. It was a masterpiece among the jade carvings in the middle of the Qing Dynasty.

19. 清乾隆青花矾红彩龙纹瓷盘

Celadon plate with the pattern of dragons in the color of iron-red, in the reign of Emperor Qianlong, the Qing Dynasty

该盘口径18厘米，底径11厘米，高4.3厘米。

Top rim diameter: 18 cm; foot rim diameter: 11 cm; height: 4.3 cm.

2008年10月绍兴市文物商店征集。

It was collected from an antique store in Shaoxing in October, 2008.

该盘为撇口，浅弧腹，矮圈足。盘内壁口沿下饰青花弦纹两周；盘心双圈升光内以青花绘海水纹为地，上为矾红彩绘一五爪龙；盘外口沿绘落花流水纹，外壁亦以青花海水纹为地，上为矾红彩绘九龙，姿态各异，腾跃于海浪之中。圈足内底书"大清乾隆年制"，青花六字三行篆书款。盘内外所绘龙头部窄平，龙眼横排，具有明代龙纹的绘画风格。乾隆时期官窑盛行仿古之风，此青花海水矾红彩龙纹盘品种，烧制始于明宣德时期，成化时期亦有制作。该盘即以宣德器为摹本，仿制而成。从整体看，此器形制轻巧，胎质细密，所绘龙纹矫健有神、气势非凡，呈现典型的乾隆时期的瓷器艺术特点。青花发色浓艳，红彩凝腻鲜亮，色彩对比鲜明，富有立体感，是一件清代乾隆官窑器的精品之作。

The plate has a spreading mouth, shallow round belly and short ringed foot. Inside the plate, the rim of the wall mouth is decorated with two rings of a blue-and-white chord pattern. In the center of the plate are two rings of rising light and its inside background is painted with the pattern of waves in blue-and-white, upon which a five-clawed dragon is drawn in the color of iron-red. Outside the plate, the rim of the wall mouth is painted with the pattern of falling blossoms and running streams and its outside background is also painted with the pattern of waves in blue-and-white, upon which nine dragons with different postures in the color of iron-red are curveting in the waves. Inside the ringed foot was written six characters "made in the reign of Emperor Qianlong in the Qing Dynasty" in three lines in seal script and blue-and-white color. Be inside or outside the plate, the dragon heads are narrow and flat, and their eyes are lined up horizontally, characterized with the painting style in the Ming Dynasty. In the reign of Emperor Qianlong, the imitation of ancient styles prevailed in the Royal Kiln. This kind of celadon plate with the pattern of dragons in the color of iron-red was fired in the reign of Emperor Xuande in the Ming Dynasty, and was also made in the reign of Emperor Chenghua. This plate was modelled after the ones in Xuande Period. As a whole, with a light structure and fine fetal materials, the painted dragons are robust, vigorous and has an extraordinary imposing manner, presenting the typical characteristics of the porcelain crafts in the reign of Emperor Qianlong. Equipped with a stereo perspective, the blue-and-white is bright-colored, and the iron-red looks solidified, fine and radiant, putting the colors in sharp contrast. It is indeed a masterpiece from the Royal Kiln during the reign of Emperor Qianlong in the Qing Dynasty.

20. 民国八年（1919年）吕公望铭鱼龙演变纹端砚
Lv Gongwang's Duan inkstone with the pattern of the evolution from carp to dragon, the eighth year of Republic of China, 1919

该砚长30厘米，宽20厘米，通高5.5厘米。

Length: 30 cm; width: 20 cm; height: 5.5 cm.

该端砚为门字形，端石质地。砚面上半部雕海水云纹，二大一小三条龙遨游其中，寓意苍龙教子。其中，小龙尾部尚处于鱼尾向龙尾的演化之中，俗称鱼龙变化或鱼化龙。从整体看，器形硕大，用料厚实，大气沉稳；雕工精湛，威龙凶猛，祥云环绕，波浪翻腾；构思精妙，布局颇具匠心。底部砚边两侧各有一列楷书刻铭，分别是"晓窗吾弟哂存 吕公望赠""民国八年镌于羊城军次（公望之印）"。吕公望，浙江永康人，字戴之。他早年加入光复会，参加过辛亥革命，曾任浙江督军兼省长。中华人民共和国成立后，他曾任浙江省政协委员。原配天地盖红木砚盒，保存至今，尤为珍贵。

The inkstone is shaped like the character "门(door)" and made of Duan stone. The top half of the inkstone surface is engraved with the cloud pattern of sea water in which three dragons, two large and one small, are swimming, with the message that the black dragons are educating their dragonet. The tail of the dragonet is still evolving from the carp one to the dragon one, known as the change between carp and dragon or the evolution from carp to dragon. Holistically speaking, its shape is quite large and its material is thick and solid, making the inkstone grand and steady; the carving crafts are delicate and a strong dragon is surrounded by auspicious clouds in the surging waves; the conception is ingenious and the layout is expertly planned. At each side on the bottom of the inkstone is respectively one engraved inscription in regular script, and they are "for my brother to keep beside the window at dawn, gifted by Lv Gongwang" and "engraved in the temporary station in Guangzhou in the 8th year of the Republic of China (Gongwang's seal)". Lv Gongwang, with the courtesy name as Daizhi, came from Yongkang, Zhejiang Province. In his early years, he joined in the Restoration Society, took part in the Revolution of 1911 and was appointed the military governor and governor of Zhejiang Province. After the founding of the People's Republic of China, he was appointed the CPPCC member of Zhejiang Province. The inkstone is originally matched with the precious up-bottom-cover redwood inkstone case, which has been preserved till now.

第七章　东阳市博物馆
Dongyang Museum

1. 中国东阳龙化石
Fossil of dinosaur, Dongyang, China

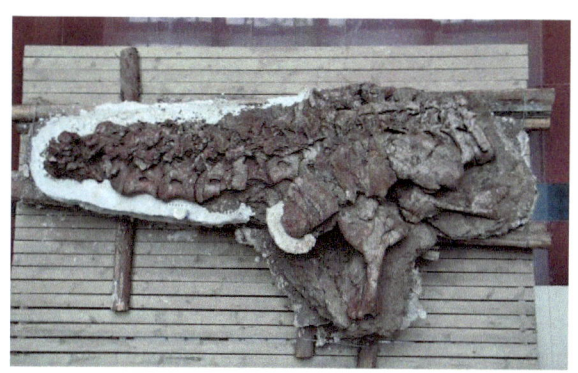

复原骨架长16米，高5米。

The structure is 16 m in length, 5 m in height.

2007年9月，此化石被发现于白云街道白殿村胡公山，保存有背椎、完整腰带和前部尾椎等。复原骨架属白垩纪巨龙科草食性蜥脚类恐龙，国际权威专业杂志《地质学报》确定它为世界上首次发现的新属新种，并正式命名为"中国东阳龙"。这意味着如果世界上其他地方发现同种恐龙化石，都将归入这个种类，也必须称之为"中国东阳龙"。东阳是一处世界罕见的恐龙骨骼、恐龙蛋和足迹化石的共生之地。

It was discovered in Hugong Mountain, Baidian Village, Baiyun Sub-district in September 2007. Back vertebra, intact waist belt and the front tail vertebra are preserved. It belongs to the Cretaceous Titanosauridae herbivorous sauropod dinosaur. *Acta Geologica Sinica*, the international authoritative and professional journal defined it as the new species discovered in the world for the first time, and named it officially "Chinese Dongyangsaurus", meaning that if the same species of dinosaur fossils are found elsewhere in the world, they will all fall into this category, and must be called "Chinese Dongyangsaurus". Dongyang is a place where dinosaur bones, dinosaur eggs and footprint fossils coexist in the world.

2. 春秋原始瓷龙纹带把杯

Primitive porcelain cup with hand at side and patterns of dragon, the Spring and Autumn Period

该器口径11.5厘米，底径10厘米，杯体高8厘米，通高10厘米。

Rim diameter: 11.5 cm; foot rim diameter: 10 cm; height of the cup: 8 cm; overall height: 10 cm.

2011年10月巍山镇西湾村缸窑山土墩墓出土。

It was unearthed in the mound tomb of Gangyao Mountain in Xiwan Village, Weishan Town in October 2011.

该杯为敛口，圆唇，直壁弧腹下收，平底。把为L型，粘于杯壁中下部。

杯体外壁刻画龙纹。杯内外施青黄釉，脱釉较严重。

It has a constricted mouth, a round lip, a straight wall and curved belly, and a flat bottom. The handle is L-shaped, being glued to the middle and lower part of the cup. The outer wall of the cup is carved with dragon patterns. Greenish yellow glazed is applied inside and outside, and the glaze has fallen down extensively.

3. 春秋玉樽

Jade goblet, the Spring and Autumn period

该器口径9.5厘米，底径11.5厘米，通高11.5厘米。

Top rim diameter: 9.5 cm; foot rim diameter: 11.5 cm; height: 11.5 cm.

2003年6月六石街道派园前山土墩墓出土。

In June 2003, it was unearthed from the mound tomb of Paiyuanqianshan in Liushi Subdistrict.

该玉樽为叶蜡石质，色以米黄为主，间杂较多细碎的白斑和大片墨绿斑，表面光滑。子母口，樽身呈直壁圆筒形，两侧口旁对称设置可活动的嵌入式四棱形装饰性耳。平底，底部有三只方形小矮足。口上有拱形盖，盖顶无钮，盖两侧有翘角形耳，耳设纵向小圆孔可与器口旁双耳上下贯通。通体光素无纹。

It is made of pyrophyllite, and it is mainly of beige in color, being mixed with many fine white spots and large dark green spots. It is smooth on surface. It has a loop mouth, a straight cylinder body, a symmetrically decorated embedded quadrangular movable ears, and a flat bottom with three little square feet. On the lid, there is an arched lid without buttons but with angled ears on its both sides. The ears are provided with longitudinal small round holes that can penetrate up and down with the ears beside the mouth of the goblet. The whole body has no lines.

4. 战国青铜甬钟
Bronze bell, the Warring States Period

该器长16.8厘米，宽12.4厘米，通高31.7厘米。

Length: 16.8 cm; width: 12.4 cm; height: 31.7 cm.

2003年城东街道李宅三江口出土。

In 2003, it was unearthed from Lizhai Sanjiangkou, Chengdong Subdistrict.

该钟腔体宽阔不长。钲部较阔，枚为三层，以小乳钉篆为间隔，分布略大于腔体的二分之一。鼓素面无纹，于较平，铣较尖。舞面饰云雷纹。甬较粗，旋部设绳纹干，衡饰云纹。

The cavity is wide and not long. The *zheng* part is relatively wide, being divided by three layers which are separated by small nails, accounting more than one-half of the cavity. The plain surface of the drum part has no patterns, the *yu* part is flat and the *xi* part is sharp. The surface is decorated with cloud and thunder patterns. *Yong* is thicker, patterned with rope on the spin part. *Heng* is decorated with clouding patterns.

5. 唐瑞禽瑞兽葡萄纹铜镜

Copper mirror with patterns of poultry, animals and grapes, the Tang Dynasty

该铜镜直径24厘米，缘高1.4厘米。

Diameter: 24 cm; rim height: 1.4 cm.

1989年6月吴宁镇爱国路李志桃捐赠。

In June 1989, it was donated by Li Zhitao of Aiguo Road, Wuning Town.

该镜呈圆形，纹饰布局分为内区、外区和镜边三部分，为圈带形式。内、外区之间用凸复线拦隔，外区与镜边用凸单线拦隔，高低起伏，层次分明。镜背以缠枝葡萄纹作地，中心饰蛙形钮。内区饰浮雕式六瑞禽六瑞兽，外区四禽四兽相间环布。镜边饰缠枝，高镜缘。镜面光滑微弧。

It takes a shape of a circle. The pattern layout in the form of a band is divided into three parts: the inner part, the outer part and the mirror rim. There designed with a convex double line to separate the inner and outer parts, a convex single line to separate the outer part and the mirror rim, forming an undulation and well-arrangement. On the back of the mirror, there designed with a grapevine pattern decorated with a frog-shaped button. The inner part is decorated with six embossed birds and beasts, while the outer part is designed with four birds and beasts. The high mirror rim is slight arched, decorated with twine patterns.

6. 唐铜鎏金男观音菩萨立像
Gilded bronze statue of standing Avalokiteshvara, the Tang Dynasty

像高15厘米。

Height: 15 cm.

1963年5月东阳南寺塔出土。

It was unearthed from Dongyang Nansi Pagoda in May 1963.

该菩萨形体清瘦，头戴宝冠，方脸男容，面带笑意。右臂下垂，手持净瓶；左臂上弯，手握柳条。身披天衣，臂绕飘带，下着罗裙，颈挂项圈，胸垂璎珞，手套腕钏，跣足立于莲台之上。莲台束腰，上饰仰莲，下为覆莲。底座八边，逐层放大。头后有一插孔，很可能是用于安装头光。造像材质为铜，通体鎏金。在我国，唐朝以前观世音的形象都是男相，直至北宋中期以后女相的观音菩萨才渐渐增多。此像即观音菩萨本为男子的有力佐证。

The thin Buddha is a square-faced man with a smile on his face, wearing a crown. His right arm is drooping, holding a *jingping* (a small vase) in his right hand; while his left arm is bent upward, holding a wicker in his left hand. He wears a heavenly robe and *luoqun* (skirt of thin silk), ribbons on his arms, a necklace of precious stones on his breast, bracelets at his wrists, being barefooted on the lotus seat. The lotus seat whose middle part is narrow is decorated with upturned lotus upside and downturned lotus downside. The octagon-shaped seat is enlarged layer by layer. At the back side of his head, there designed with a hole probably for a backlight. The statue is made of copper and gilded throughout. Before the Tang Dynasty in our country, the image of Guanyin was male. It was not until the mid-

North Song Dynasty that the female Guanyin Bodhisattva gradually increased. This status is a powerful proof that Guanyin Bodhisattva is a man.

7. 唐婺州窑青瓷海水纹折腹钵
Celadon glazed alms bowl with seawater patterns of Wuzhou kiln, the Tang Dynasty

该器口径14.4厘米,底径7.5厘米,高17.7厘米。

Top rim diameter: 14.4 cm; bottom rim diameter: 7.5 cm; height: 17.7 cm.

1993年6月北江镇木塘头村出土。

It was unearthed in Mutangtou Village, Beijiang Town, June 1993.

该钵为敛口圆唇,折腹弧收,圈足内凹。外表上腹饰一周波浪卷草纹,内表下腹饰旋涡纹。内外施青釉,釉面均匀,布细裂纹。胎质灰白,保存完整。

The mouth is rounded, the belly is folded, and the foot is concave. The upper belly on the outside is decorated with a wavy grass pattern, and the lower belly on the inner surface is decorated with a swirl pattern. Celadon glaze is applied inside and outside, and the glaze is even, being patterned with capillary crack. The carcass is gray and white, and is preserved intact.

8. 五代绿色琉璃壶

Green glaze pot, the Five Dynasties

该壶高7.8厘米。

Height: 7.8 cm.

1963年5月东阳南寺塔出土。

It was unearthed in Dongyang Nansi Pagoda, May 1963.

该琉璃壶为敞口，平沿宽唇，细束颈。壶体扁圆形，底部内凹。品质晶莹剔透，色彩均匀，呈绿中带蓝色。此壶采用高温脱蜡铸造法制成，造型规整，制作精致。

It is oblate-shaped, with an open mouth, a flat rim, a wide lip, narrow neck and a concave bottom. It is crystal clear and evenly colored. There is green in blue. It is made through a dewaxing casting method in a high temperature. It is regular shaped and delicate produced.

9. 五代花鸟纹金舍利盒

Buddhist relic box with golden patterns of birds and flowers, the Five Dynasties

该盒直径2.5厘米，通高1厘米。

Diameter: 2.5 cm; overall height: 1 cm.

1963年5月东阳南市塔出土。

It was unearthed in Dongyang Nanshi Pagoda in May 1963.

该盒呈扁体圆形，器盖器身以子母口盖合，盖面身底均作弧形凸起，盖面錾刻朱雀花枝，底面錾刻重瓣宝相花。此盒制作精致，保存完整，用于存放舍利子。

The box is flat and round, and the body of the lid is closed with a loop mouth. The bottom of the lid and the bottom of the body are all arc-shaped protrusions. The surface of the lid is patterned with *zhuque* (vermillion birds) and sprays, while the surface of the bottom is patterned with po-phase flowers. It is exquisitely crafted and preserved intact, being used to store Buddhist relics.

10. 五代铜鎏金阿育王塔
Gilded copper Ashoka pagoda, the Five Dynasties

该塔底长16.5厘米，宽16.6厘米，通高38.6厘米。

Length: 16.5 cm; width: 16.6 cm; overall height: 38.6 cm.

该塔为方形，由基座、塔身、塔顶三部分组成，通体铜质，外表鎏金。基座为方形，须弥座式，束腰四面各铸有四尊结跏趺坐佛像。基座上表面开有八个长方形孔，四角四孔用于安装塔身，中间四孔安插佛像。塔身为方形，四面拱形龛内镂刻摩诃萨埵太子舍身饲虎、月光王施宝首、尸毗王割肉贸鸽、快目王舍眼四幅佛本生故事画面，四角各立一护法大鹏金翅鸟。

The pagoda is square, composing of a base, a pagoda body, and a pagoda top. It is made of copper with gilded surface outside. The base is square, styled with Sumeru. At the four sides of the waist part, there casted four Buddha images sitting cross-legged. On the base, there set eight rectangular holes, four of them are for the pagoda body while the other four are for Buddha images. The pagoda body is square, whose four sides are inscribed with four stories: the Prince Mahasattva sacrificed himself to feed the tiger, the King Moonlight devoted his head, King Shipi cut his flesh for the pigeon and King Sudhira sacrificed his eyes. On the four corners, there stand four Garuda respectively.

塔身的最上层用忍冬及兽面纹作装饰。塔身四角的山花蕉叶、正面的镂空图案为反映佛祖一生事迹的佛传故事画面，共16幅；背面的图案为佛坐禅、说法等形象。塔刹由刹杆、五重相轮和火焰宝珠等构成，塔刹的底座装饰八瓣覆莲，五重相轮底轮最大，往上渐收。此塔保存基本完整。1963年5月于东阳城南勒马峰北麓倒塌后的南寺塔发掘出土，现藏于东阳市博物馆。

The top part of the pagoda body is decorated with honey suckle and beast patterns. The pediments and banana leaves at the four corners of the body as well as the hollow patterns on the front of the body tell the Buddha's life story, totaling 16 scenes. The design on the back is the scenes of Buddha sitting in meditation or delivering statement. The pagoda spire consists of pole, quadruple wheels and flaming bright pearls. The base of the pagoda is decorated with a down-turned lotus with eight petals. The wheel is increasingly large from the bottom to the top. The pagoda is kept intact. In May 1963, it was excavated from the Nansi Pagoda after the collapse of the north foot of Lema Peak in the south of Dongyang City. It is now in the Dongyang Museum.

根据题记，此鎏金塔为吴越国民间铸造，它反映了普通信众的信仰与祈愿。此塔较一般的阿育王塔要大，甚至比常见的官方造阿育王塔还大。此塔制作精致，体现出吴越国铜器制作的工艺水平，对研究吴越国时期佛教文化具有重要价值。

According to the inscription, this gilded pagoda was cast by Wuyue folks, reflecting the beliefs and wishes of the public. This pagoda is larger than the general Ashoka pagodas, and even larger than the common official Ashoka pagodas. It is exquisitely made, representing the craftsmanship of the bronze ware making in the Wuyue Kingdom. It is of great value for studying Buddhist culture of the Wuyue Kingdom.

阿育王塔因印度孔雀王朝第三代国王阿育王而得名。据史料记载，公元前3世纪，统一印度的阿育王皈依佛教后，派遣僧侣四方传播佛教，还取出王舍城大宝塔阿阇世王分得的佛陀舍利，并将其分成八万四千份，在世界各地供奉佛舍利。这些舍利用小塔供养，因盛舍利的小塔系阿育王下令建造，故称"阿育王塔"。五代十国时期，吴越国王钱弘俶崇奉佛教，效法古印度阿育王，也命人造塔，广推佛教。此塔虽非官方所造，但其造型和图案内容与同时期的官方造塔一致，习惯上也将其称为阿育王塔。

The Pagoda is named after Ashoka, the third king of the Maurya Dynasty in India. According to historical records, in the 3rd century BC, King Ashoka, who unified India, converted to Buddhism and sent monks to spread Buddhism. He also took out the Buddha relics distributed by King Ajan, the great pagoda of Wangshecheng, and divided them into 84,000 copies for people to enshrine and worship all over the world. The Buddha relics are enshrined and worshipped in small pagodas. Because the small pagodas were built by the order of King Ashoka, they were called "Ashoka Towers". During the Five Dynasties and Ten Kingdoms Period, Qian Hongchu, the king of Wuyue, worshipped Buddhism, imitating the ancient Indian King Ashoka, and ordered man-made pagodas to promote Buddhism. Although this pagoda is not officially built, its shape and pattern content are consistent with the official ones of the same period, and it is customarily called the Ashoka Tower.

11. 五代木雕罗汉像
Wood statue of monks, the Five Dynasties

该像底宽4.2厘米，半径2.9厘米，通高18.8厘米。

Width: 4.2 cm; radius: 2.9 cm; height: 18.8 cm.

1963年5月东阳南寺塔出土。

It was unearthed in Dongyang Nansi Pagoda, May 1963.

该罗汉像为光头圆脸，眉目修长，鼻梁高挺，面颊丰满，嘴唇微张，双耳垂肩。像身着袈裟，双手合十，跣足立在钵形状、复线双层仰莲纹莲台上。像身后设龛，身与龛之间有一窄缝。龛体上部垂叠层帷幔，下部设须弥座。上枋雕双线仰莲纹，束腰刻壸门，下枋和圭脚饰以凸条纹，龛壁两侧阴刻折线纹。像、龛比例适中，重心稳定，由一块木头雕刻而成。底座平面近1/4圆形。此像是东阳木雕中现存最早和保存最完整的历史实物，对研究东阳木雕文化具有重要意义。

The figure has a bald head, a round face, slender eyebrows, a high nose and plump cheeks, with a lip slightly opening, double ears drooping on shoulders. He wears kasaya, with hands folded, barefooted standing on the up-turned lotus base shaped bowl and patterned with double lines. There is a niche behind the statue, with a narrow gap between the body and the niche. The upper part of the niche is covered with a draped curtain, and the lower part is equipped with a sacred seat. The upper arch is carved with a double-line upturned lotus pattern, the waist is carved with a pot gate, and the lower arch and feet are decorated with convex stripes. Both sides of the niche wall are inscribed with broken lines. The statue and the niche are of moderate proportions, with a stable center of gravity, and are carved from a piece of wood. The base plane is nearly 1/4 circular. This statue is the earliest and most complete historical object of Dongyang Woodcarving, which is of great significance to the study of Dongyang woodcarving culture.

12. 宋婺州窑青瓷莲瓣纹盖罐

Celadon pot of Wuzhou kiln with cap in design of lotus petals, the Song Dynasty

该罐口径5.8厘米，底径7.7厘米，通高9.6厘米。

Top rim diameter: 5.8 cm; bottom rim diameter: 7.7 cm; height: 9.6 cm.

2009年9月白云街道杨大金交椅山宋墓出土。

In September 2009, it was unearthed from the Song Tomb of Jiaoyi Mountain, Yang Dajin, Baiyun Subdistrict.

该罐体为鼓形，敛口，圆鼓腹。外壁刻五层莲瓣纹，下为喇叭形圈足。盖为子母口，平圆形，上表面刻二层莲瓣纹，中心粘饰蜗牛壳形钮。罐、盖均施青釉。

The pot body is in the shape of a drum, with a constricted mouth and a round belly. The outer wall is engraved with five layers of lotus petals, and the bottom is a flared ring. The cover is a loop, flat and round, with a double-lotus-petal pattern on the upper surface, and a snail shell-shaped button attached to the center. The celadon glaze is applied to the jar and lid.

13. 宋婺州窑青瓷菊瓣纹粉盒

Celadon compact of Wuzhou kiln with design of chrysanthemum petals, the Song Dynasty

该盒口径8.8厘米，底径4.6厘米，通高5.2厘米。

Rim diameter: 8.8 cm; bottom rim diameter: 4.6 cm; height: 5.2 cm.

1995年5月歌山镇歌山窑址出土。

In May 1995, it was unearthed in the Geshan Kiln site of Geshan Town.

该盒形似橘子，子母口。器盖中部有圆凸弦纹两圈，中心置S型带钩状盖钮。盖面刻画菊瓣纹，器身与盖同高，尖圆唇，直子口下腹圆弧内收。胎质灰白，内外施青釉，玻璃质强。

It looks like an orange with a loop mouth. There are two round convex string patterns in the middle of the lid, the center is set with an S-shaped hook-like lid button, the lid surface is engraved with chrysanthemum petals, and the body and the lid are the same height. The pointed round lip, the straight mouth and the lower belly are curved inward. The fetus is gray and white, with celadon glaze on the inside and outside. It has a strong sense of glass.

14. 宋长方形麻质蓝印花布

Blue rectangle flax calico, the Song Dynasty

该布长160厘米，宽40厘米。

Length: 160 cm; width: 40 cm.

2000年2月南马镇南田村太平山出土。

In February 2000, it was unearthed from Taiping Mountain in Nantian Village, Nanma Town.

长方形布块，为麻料织品，纵横上下交叉编织。蓝底白花，以连续铜钱纹作地，间杂葵形开光花卉、圆形开光花卉、八边形开光花卉等图案，菊花、团花以及其他不知名的花排列间杂有序。布块蓝白色彩分明。局部有朽烂缺损。

This rectangular cloth, made of linen fabric, is woven vertically and horizontally. With white flowers on a blue background, with a continuous copper-coin pattern as the ground, it has patterns of sunflower-shaped consecrated flowers, round consecrated flowers, octagonal consecrated flowers and others. There are chrysanthemums, cluster flowers and other unknown flowers, arranged in an orderly arrangement. The blue and white colors of the cloth are distinct. However, there is partial defect.

15. 宋银边三层漆脱胎

Lacquer case with three silver lining, the Song Dynasty

该器口径16.3厘米，底径16.3厘米，高13.8厘米。

Top rim diameter: 16.3 cm; bottom rim diameter: 16.3 cm; height: 13.8 cm.

2000年2月南马镇南田村太平山出土。

In February 2000, it was unearthed from Taiping Mountain in Nantian Village, Nanma Town.

该器为圆筒形，篾质夹纻胎，由盖（残）、底及套装在底口之上的两层深浅不一的盘组成。它为三层漆奁，每层各镶银箍，其中一、二层各三道，底层二道。器物内外髹以黑漆，为镶、箍、漆等多种工艺相结合的漆器。

It takes a shape of cylinder, made of thin bamboo stripes and linen. It consists of a cover (or cover remnant), a bottom, and two plates of different depths on the bottom. It is a three-layer lacquer case, each of layer is inlaid with silver loops. In particular, the first and second layer have three lines respectively, and the bottom layer has two lines. The inside and outside of the ware are painted with black lacquer, which is a combination of inlay, hoop, lacquer and other techniques.

16. 宋木质夹纻胎漆盘

Lacquer plate made of wood and ramie, the Song Dynasty

该器口径24.7厘米，底径17.6厘米，高6.7厘米。

Top rim diameter: 24.7 cm; bottom rim diameter: 17.6 cm; height: 6.7 cm.

2000年2月南马镇南田村太平山出土。

In February 2000, it was unearthed from Taiping Mountain in Nantian Village, Nanma Town.

该盘为敛口，圆弧腹下收，平底内凹，圈足，篾质夹纻胎。口及口沿镶以银箍一道，稍向外卷。器物内壁髹朱红漆，并有凹弦纹一圈；外壁及底足髹黑漆。

It has a constricted mouth, a retracted belly, a flat concave bottom and circled feet. It was made of thin bamboo stripes and linen. There is a silver hoop inlaid on the mouth and rim, slightly rolled outwards. The inner wall is painted with vermilion lacquer, with a circle of concave string patterns; the outer wall and bottom of the foot are painted with black lacquer.

17. 宋双鱼龙耳金杯

Gold goblet with dragon-shaped handles at sides, the Song Dynasty

该器口径6.2厘米，底径2.8厘米，高5.3厘米。

Top rim diameter: 6.2 cm; bottom rim diameter: 2.8 cm; height: 5.3 cm.

2009年11月白云街道杨大金交椅山宋墓出土。

In November 2009, it was unearthed from the Song Tomb of Yang Dajin Jiaoyi Mountain in Baiyun Subdistrict.

该杯为侈口，尖唇，微束颈，直壁弧腹，腹下为喇叭形圈足。双耳对称，饰鱼龙。杯外壁錾刻圆形双鸟图案，图案均匀分布，内底錾刻龙纹。器物造型独特，通体金质，色泽金黄。

It has a bigger mouth, pointed lip, slightly narrowed neck, straight wall and curved belly under which there is a trumpet-shaped ring foot. The ears are symmetrical, decorated with ichthyosaurs. The outer wall of the cup is engraved with a circular double-bird pattern, evenly distributed, and the inner bottom is engraved with a dragon pattern. The cup is unique in shape, made of gold overall. Therefore, it is golden yellow.

18. 宋银鎏金双龙戏珠纹盏托

Gilded silver lamp base with design of two dragons frolicking with a pearl, the Song Dynasty

该器口径14.6厘米，底径11.5厘米，高1厘米。

Top rim diameter: 14.6 cm; bottom rim diameter: 11.5 cm; height: 1 cm.

2009年11月白云街道杨大金交椅山宋墓出土。

In November 2009, it was unearthed from the Song Tomb of Yang Dajin Jiaoyi Mountain in Baiyun Subdistrict.

该器为圆盘形，宽沿，浅腹，平底。口沿錾刻卷草纹。盘心稍低于盘面，錾刻双龙戏珠，外周为凸起的托圈。盘面捶揲两条海水龙纹。盏托表面鎏金。此盏托与金杯系一套金银酒器。

It takes a shape of a round plate, with wide rim, shallow belly and flat bottom. The rim of the mouth is carved with curly grass patterns. The center of the base is slightly lower than the surface, engraved with patters of double dragons frolicking with pearl, and the outer periphery is decorated with two sea-dragon patterns. The surface is gilded. This base and the gold cup is a set of gold and silver wine vessel.

19. 宋银鎏金云龙纹瓶

Gilded silver vase with patterns of dragons and clouds, the Song Dynasty

该瓶口径4.9厘米，底径7.3厘米，高13.8厘米。

Top rim diameter: 4.9 cm; bottom rim diameter: 7.3 cm; height: 13.8 cm.

该瓶为圆唇，口微侈，长直颈，平肩，腹部微鼓，圈足。颈部錾刻两条在云海中升腾的螭龙，腹部錾刻两条游动的螭龙，圈足錾刻一周云龙纹，肩部錾刻海水纹，近腹部与近足处均錾刻一周乳丁纹。底部錾刻"口五郎"字样。

It has a round lip, with a slightly exaggerated mouth, long straight neck, flat shoulders, slightly bulging belly, and ringed foot. The neck is carved with two *chilong* (a kind of ancient dragon in China) rising in the sea of clouds, the belly is carved with two swimming *chilong*, the ringed feet are carved with a circle of a cloud dragon pattern, and the shoulders are carved with seawater patterns. There is a circle of nails decorated around the belly and foot respectively. At the bottom, there engraved characters of "kouwulang".

20. 北宋婺州窑"天圣六年造自使也"铭瓷碾轮
Porcelain runner wheel with inscriptions of "made in the sixth year of Tiansheng Period for private use" in the Wuzhou kiln, the Northern Song Dynasty

轮径11.4厘米，轮厚2.5厘米，中心圆孔直径2.1厘米。

Diameter: 11.4 cm; thickness: 2.5 cm; diameter of the central hole: 2.1 cm.

1980年歌山马龙山窑址出土。

It was unearthed from the Malongshan Kiln Site in Geshan in 1980.

碾轮为瓷质，形如铁饼，外缘薄、内里厚，弧面，中间开圆孔。顺时针方向阴刻"天圣六年造自使也"铭文，字体为行书。表面未施釉，呈灰红色。

It is made of porcelain, shaped like a discus, with a thin outer rim and thick inside, and with a curved surface and a round hole in the middle. It is inscribed clockwise with "tianshengliunianzaozishiye" in running script. The surface is not glazed, and is grayish red.

21. 南宋水晶如意饰件
Crystal *ruyi*, the Southern Song Dynasty

该器长7.2厘米，横5.8厘米，厚1.2厘米。

Length: 7.2 cm; width: 5.8 cm; thickness: 1.2 cm.

1982年湖溪镇罗青甲南宋墓出土。

It was unearthed from the Southern Song Dynasty Tomb of Luo Qingjia in Huxi Town in 1982.

饰件呈椭圆形，中间镂空，形似如意，左右对称，做工精致。一侧晶莹光洁透亮，另一侧略带茶色，似有几抹飘云淡雾，别具灵动之气。

This ornament is oval in shape, with a hollow in the middle, resembling a shape of *ruyi* (an S-shaped ornamental object, usually made of jade, formerly a symbol of good luck). It is bilaterally symmetrical. With exquisite workmanship, one side is crystal clear and translucent, and the other side is slightly brown, seeming to be a few wispy clouds and mist, which is unique and agile.

22. 南宋鸳鸯纹金帔坠

Gold pendant with design of mandarin ducks, the Southern Song Dynasty

该器长7.9厘米，横7.1厘米，重35克。

Length: 7.9 cm; width: 7.1 cm; weight: 35 g.

1984年5月湖溪镇罗青甲砖瓦厂出土，何贤木上交。

In May 1984, it was unearthed from the brick and tile factory in Luoqingjia, Huxi Town, and was handed in by He Xianmu.

坠似心形，图案左右对称。鸳鸯蹼踩莲蓬，展翅平衡，后尾上翘化为缠枝蜿绕，动静结合，趣意盎然。中间结带，上为花结，下垂三环。坠经捶揲、錾刻、拼合而成，正反面相同，工艺精致。

The pendant is shaped like a heart, with symmetrical patterns. There designed with mandarin ducks stepping on the lotus to spread their wings in balance. The rear tails of mandarin ducks are upturned into winding branches, presenting a dynamic and static effect, which is full of fun. The middle knot has a rosette on the top, and three loops drooping down. The pendant is hammered, engraved, and assembled. The front and back are the same, showing exquisite craftsmanship.

第八章　永康市博物馆
Yongkang Museum

1. 南朝婺州窑青瓷羊首壶
Goat-headed celadon glazed pot of Wuzhou kiln, the Southern Dynasty

该壶口径8.4厘米，内径6厘米，外底径8.8厘米，高27.5厘米。

Top rim diameter: 8.4 cm; inner diameter 6 cm; outer bottom diameter: 8.8 cm; height: 27.5 cm.

该壶盘口微侈，外饰弦纹，溜肩，圆腹，假圈足外撇内凹。肩两侧各饰一对桥形系。口肩之间设有龙形柄；龙头双角卷曲，衔于壶口；柄弯垂于肩，流为羊头状。龙头与羊头一前一后，相视成趣，形象生动。器物胎体灰色，质地坚实，底足露胎，施青绿色釉。此壶造型优美，釉质润亮，纹饰朴实简练，难得一见。

The handicap is slightly exaggerated, with a string pattern on the outside. It has slipped shoulders, round belly, and false ring feet flinging outside and concave inside. A pair of bridges are on each side of the shoulder. There is a dragon-shaped handle between the mouth and shoulders. The double horns of the faucet are curled and hung on the mouth of the pot. The handle is bent over the shoulders and flows like a sheep's head. The dragon-shaped head and the sheep-shaped head present a funny look at each other. It is gray, solid in texture, with exposed feet and green glaze. It is rarely to see this beautiful shape, smooth glaze, simple and concise decoration.

2. 唐照日菱花四兽青铜镜
Zhaori bronze mirror with patterns of diamonds and four beasts, the Tang Dynasty

该铜镜直径10.3厘米，边厚0.9厘米。

Diameter: 10.3 cm; rim thickness: 0.9 cm.

该镜为青铜质，圆形，圆钮，圆钮座。主题纹为四瑞兽在草地上奔驰。此镜以双凸弦纹隆起相隔，分内外二区，使镜面高低起伏、错落有致。内区高圆浮雕瑞兽四只，体态丰腴柔健，活泼生动。兽间以花草，往外为锯齿纹和辐射纹。外区为铭文带。此镜乌黑发亮，立体感强，富丽大方。唐代的铜镜在造型上，除了继续沿用之前的圆形、方形之外，又创造了菱花式的纹镜，并且把反映人们对理想的追求和对幸福生活的向往的画面应用到镜上。此镜题材新颖，纹饰华美，精工细致，堪称唐代精品。

The bronze mirror takes a shape of a circle, with round button and round button base. The theme pattern is four auspicious beast running on the grass. Separate by the double convex string patterns, the mirror was divided into inner and outer areas, making mirror surface well-proportioned. In the inner area, there are four beasts in high-circle relief, plump, soft and lively. Among the beasts, there are flowers and plants, with sawtooth patterns and radiation patterns outwards. The outer area is the inscription belt. This mirror is black and shiny, rich and generous, showing a strong three-dimensional effect. In terms of the shape of the bronze mirror in the Tang Dynasty, there were diamond-shaped mirrors besides the previous round and square mirrors. In addition, the scenes of people in pursuit of ideals, auspiciousness and happiness were applied into mirrors. This mirror has novel themes, gorgeous decorations, and meticulous workmanship. It can be regarded as a boutique in the Tang Dynasty.

3. 中生代鱼化石
Mesozoic fish fossil

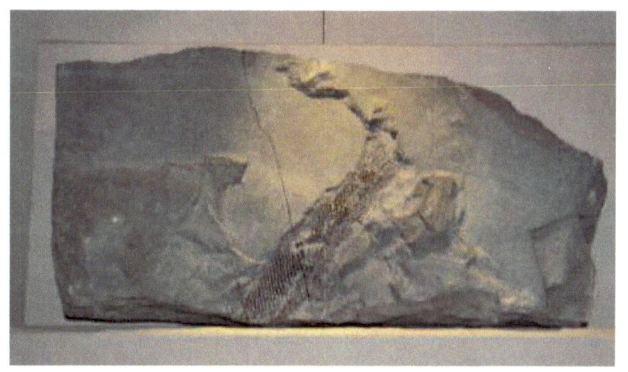

该化石长74厘米，宽35.4厘米，高15厘米。

Length: 74 cm; width: 35.4 cm; height: 15 cm.

4. 新石器时代石箭镞
Neolithic stone arrowheads

该器纵长7.1厘米，宽1.5厘米，厚0.3厘米。
Length: 7.1 cm; width: 1.5 cm; thickness: 0.3 cm.

5. 新石器时代石磨棒
Neolithic axe

该棒长10厘米，宽5.4厘米，厚4厘米。

Length: 10 cm; width: 5.4 cm; thickness: 4 cm.

6. 西周酱釉S纹原始瓷豆

Brownish-purple glazed primitive porcelain Dou (lamp) with S-shaped patterns, the Western Zhou Dynasty

该器口径8.5厘米，足径7厘米，高7.2厘米。

Top rim diameter: 8.5 cm; bottom rim diameter: 7 cm; height: 7.2 cm.

7. 战国短腊斜从有格剑

Sword with stick, short handles and tilt blade, the Warring States Period

该剑纵长39.3厘米，厚0.9厘米。

Length: 39.3 cm; thickness: 0.9 cm.

8. 汉鎏金铜镜残件
Relic of gilded copper mirror, the Han Dynasty

该件长95厘米，宽23厘米，高5厘米。

Length: 95 cm; width: 23 cm; height: 5 cm.

9. 东汉龙虎铜镜
Bronze mirror with patterns of dragon and tiger, the Eastern Han Dynasty

该铜镜直径13.5厘米，边厚0.1厘米。

Diameter: 13.5 cm; thickness: 0.1 cm.

10. 东汉婺州窑青瓷虎子
Celadon Huzi of Wuzhou kiln, the Eastern Han Dynasty

该器口径4.9厘米，底径27.5厘米，高18.2厘米。

Top rim diameter: 4.9 cm; bottom rim diameter: 27.5 cm; height: 18.2 cm.

11. 三国青瓷瓮
Celadon jar, the Three Kingdoms Period

该器口径23.5厘米，底径20.5厘米，高35厘米。

Top rim diameter: 23.5 cm; bottom rim diameter: 20.5 cm; height: 35 cm.

12. 西晋青瓷鬼灶
Celadon kitchen, the Western Jin Dynasty

该器纵19.2厘米，横16.5厘米，高14厘米。

Length: 19.2 cm; width: 16.5 cm; height: 14 cm.

13. 西晋婺州窑青瓷谷仓
Celadon granary of Wuzhou kiln, the Western Jin Dynasty

该器口径31.2厘米，底径17.1厘米，通高41.5厘米。

Top rim diameter: 31.2 cm; bottom rim diameter: 17.1 cm; height: 41.5 cm.

14. 宋四体诗文端砚

Inkstone made by Duan stone carved with poems on four sides, the Song Dynasty

该砚纵长17.8厘米,宽11.2厘米,高4.3厘米。

Length: 17.8 cm; width: 11.2 cm; height: 4.3 cm.

15. 宋如意形白玉饰件

White jade Ruyi shaped accessory, the Song Dynasty

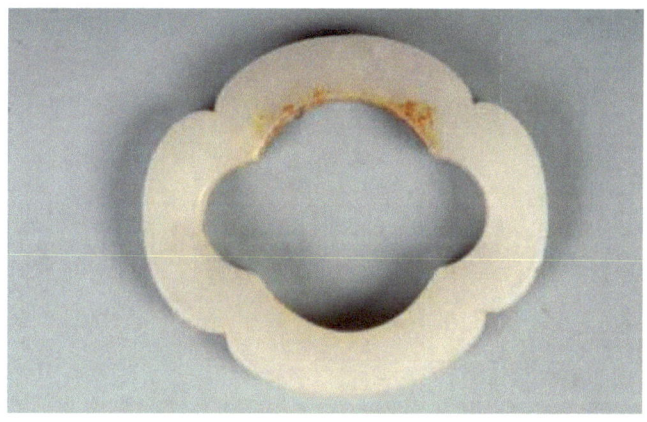

该器长5.1厘米,宽4.4厘米,高0.5厘米。

Length: 5.1 cm; width: 4.4 cm; height: 0.5 cm.

16. 宋葵形湖州铜镜
Copper flowered-shaped mirror of Huzhou, the Song Dynasty

该铜镜直径7厘米，厚0.2厘米。

Diameter: 7 cm; thickness: 0.2 cm.

17. 北宋婺州窑青瓷粉盒
Celadon compact of Wuzhou kiln, the Northern Song Dynasty

该盒口径12.2厘米，通高5.2厘米。

Top rim diameter: 12.2 cm; height: 5.2 cm.

18. 北宋婺州窑青瓷堆纹瓶

Celadon pot with modeled figured of Wuzhou kiln, the Northern Song Dynasty

该瓶口径9厘米，底径10.3厘米，通高38厘米。

Top rim diameter: 9 cm; bottom rim diameter: 10.3 cm; height: 38 cm.

19. 北宋青瓷刻花大碗

Celadon bowl with carved patterns, the Northern Song Dynasty

该碗口径16厘米，足径5.4厘米，高7.5厘米。

Top rim diameter: 16 cm; bottom rim diameter: 5.4 cm; height: 7.5 cm.

20. 元龙泉窑青瓷大碗
Celadon bowl of Longquan kiln, the Yuan Dynasty

该碗口径16.8厘米，足径7厘米，高7厘米。

Top rim diameter: 16.8 cm; bottom rim diameter: 7 cm; height: 7 cm.

21. 元婺州窑乳浊釉盖罐
Opacified glazed pot of Wuzhou kiln, the Yuan Dynasty

该罐口径7厘米，底径4.2厘米，通高11.2厘米。

Top rim diameter: 7 cm; bottom rim diameter: 4.2 cm; height: 11.2 cm.

22. 明祭蓝釉瓷瓶
Blue glazed pot, the Ming Dynasty

该瓶口径2.8厘米，足径3.5厘米，通高6.5厘米。

Top rim diameter: 2.8 cm; foot rim diameter: 3.5 cm; height: 6.5 cm.

23. 清景德镇窑粉彩《红楼梦》人物盖罐
Pink-colored covered jar with patterns of figures in *A Dream in Red Masions* made in Jingdezhen kiln, the Qing Dynasty

该罐口径9.2厘米，底径17厘米，通高20.5厘米。

Top rim diameter: 9.2 cm; bottom rim diameter: 17 cm; height: 20.5 cm.

24. 清朱砂砚
Cinnabar ink stone, the Qing Dynasty

该砚长14.8厘米，宽8.9厘米，高1.9厘米。

Length: 14.8 cm; width: 8.9 cm; height: 1.9 cm.

25. 清镂雕蝶恋花玉饰件
Jade with hollowed pattern of butterfly loving flower, the Qing Dynasty

该件长8.2厘米，宽5.7厘米，厚0.3厘米。

Length: 8.2 cm; width: 5.7 cm; height: 0.3 cm.

26. 清龙川文集木雕版
Carving board of the collective works of Longchuan, the Qing Dynasty

该木雕版长28.5厘米，宽19.0厘米，厚2.4厘米。

Length: 28.5 cm; width: 19 cm; height: 2.4 cm.

27. 民国时期花鸟纹刺绣肚兜
Bellyband embroidered with patterns of flowers and birds, the Republic of China (1912—1949)

该肚兜最长30厘米，最宽30厘米。

Max length: 30 cm; max width: 30 cm.

第九章　武义县博物馆
Wuyi Museum

1. 三国伎乐俑五管瓶
Five-tube bottle designed with figurines, the Three Kingdoms

三国伎乐俑五管瓶釉色温润，造型奇特，运用了捏塑、模印、刻画等多种装饰手法，将胡人形象刻画得栩栩如生；外施青褐色釉不及底且肩部及腹部垂

釉明显，胎釉结合良好，厚实滋润，是武义婺州窑最具代表性的堆塑精品。

The five-tube bottle has a warm glaze and a peculiar shape. It uses a variety of decorative techniques such as kneading, moulding, and carving to portray the image of the Hu people vividly; the cyan glaze applied outside was not obvious as that on bottom, shoulders and belly part. The carcass and the glaze is well combined, being thick and moist. It is the most representative modeled product of Wuyi Wuzhou kiln.

这两件三国伎乐俑五管瓶，一件为男俑（左），另一件为女俑（右），应为一对。武义县博物馆于1995年将两件物品出借给上海博物馆，上海博物馆为其单设中心展柜，长期展出。2019年3月，武义县博物馆新馆落成，收回一件男俑五管瓶，放置于婺州窑专题陈列中展出。

Among the two five-tube bottles of figurines in the Three Kingdoms, one is a male figurine (left) and the other is a female figurine (right). They should be a pair. Wuyi Museum lent them to Shanghai Museum in 1995, and Shanghai Museum set up a single central showcase for them for a long-term exhibition. In March 2019, the new Wuyi Museum was completed, and one piece of them (the male figurine) was taken back and put in the special exhibition of Wuzhou Kiln.

男俑五管瓶，器身高42厘米、腹径22厘米、底径12厘米。瓶身呈葫芦形，上塑五管，中心管较大，4根小管围绕中心管分布，5根管体与器腹相通，外形呈胡人形象。中心管胡人形象着阔幅短袖，凹脸高鼻，浓眉大眼，且腮部刻有胡须，做吹毕栗（古代一种管乐器）状。中心管前方2根小管塑造的胡人形象，右侧一个做吹排箫状，左侧一个做双手打节拍状。器物肩部一周堆塑人物5个，动物3只。

The five-tube bottle of male figurines is 42 cm in height, 22 cm in middle rim and 12 cm in bottom diameter. The bottle is in the shape of a gourd, with five modeled tubes. The center tube is larger, and the other four are small tubes being distributed around the center tube. They all connect with the body. The figurine is Hu-people alike. The Hu figurine of the center tube is wearing a coat with broad short sleeves. He has a concave face, a high nose, thick eyebrows and big eyes, and a beard on the cheeks, with a gesture of playing bili (an ancient wind instrument). For the two Hu-people shaped small tubes, one on the right side is playing a panpipe, and the other on the left side is clapping hands. There are 5 figures and 3 animals around the shoulder of the relic.

女俑五管瓶，器身高36.6厘米、腹径22.4厘米、底径12厘米。中心管的胡人形象，同样着阔幅短袖，凹脸高鼻。不同的是其面部清秀，怀抱一婴儿于胸前，抚面贴脸，做哺乳状。边上4根为素管，前2根管中间跪着2人，做仆人状。下一层正面有1人做倒立状，左边上2人做拍手状；一周共有动物4只，其憨态可掬，形象生动。

The five-tube bottle of female figurines is 36.6 cm in height, 22.4 cm in belly rim diameter and 12 cm in bottom rim diameter. The Hu figurine of the center tube is wearing a coat with broad short sleeves. She has a concave face and a high nose while a delicate and pretty face. She holds an infant in front of her breast, touching her face while breast-breading. The other four tubes are plain, and there are two people kneeling in the middle of the first two pipes, acting like servants. On the front of the lower layer, there is one figurine standing upside down, and two figurines on the left side clapping hands. There are four animals around, charming and lively.

2. 宋湖田窑青白瓷执壶

Hutian bluish white glazed porcelain pot with a handle, the Song Dynasty

该壶通高15.7厘米，口径6.5厘米，底径9.3厘米。

It is 15.7 cm in height, 6.5 cm in diameter, and 9.3 cm in bottom diameter.

宋代，景德镇瓷器烧造技艺日益精进，仿效青白玉的色调和温润的质感，创烧出青白瓷。其胎质细腻洁白，釉面光亮，釉色白中泛青，在刻有暗花的地方呈现浅淡的青绿色，因此也称"影青"；又因其釉色类似玉，有"饶玉"的美称。

In the Song Dynasty, the porcelain firing skills in Jingdezhen became more and more refined. Basing on the tone and the warm texture of light greenish white jade, it was to create the bluish white porcelain with delicate and white texture, bright glaze in blue and white. The light blue green appeared in the area carved with floral patterns, which was endowed with the name of "*yingqing* (misty blue)". It was also named "raoyu (rich jade)", for its jade-like glaze.

景德镇青白瓷在武义县出土数量多。1976年，武义岩坞村北宋元丰墓出土陶瓷器共17件，其中有执壶、荷叶形碗、折沿浅碟、芒口碟等青白瓷。这说明随着宋代武义茶叶生产的发展和饮茶之风的兴起，当时景德镇生产的瓷器尤其是茶具，已经在武义人的日常生活中被普遍使用。

Many Jingdezhen bluish white porcelains were unearthed in Wuyi County. In 1976, a total of 17 ceramics were unearthed from the Yuanfeng Tomb of the Northern Song Dynasty in Yanwu Village, Wuyi County, including bluish white porcelains such as pots with handles, lotus leaf-shaped bowls, folded edge shallow dishes, and Mangkou dishes, showing that the porcelain produced in Jingdezhen at that time, especially tea sets, had been widely used in the daily life of Wuyi people with the development of tea production and the rise of tea drinking in Wuyi in the Song Dynasty.

这件青白瓷执壶，产自景德镇烧制青白瓷最重要的窑址——湖田窑。器盖内凹，与口沿相合，下凹处有一小尖钮。口沿外翻，颈粗短，圆鼓腹，流向上弧伸。肩部饰一扁条状执柄，执柄上近口沿处与器盖各有一对应的孔，可用绳系。胎体洁白细腻，釉色明亮，白中闪青，开细片。其造型典雅，制作精巧，堪称精品。

This blue-white glazed porcelain pot was produced in Hutian Kiln, the most important kiln site for firing bluish white porcelain in Jingdezhen. The lid of the device is recessed to meet the edge of the mouth, and there is a small sharp button in the lower recess. The rim of the mouth is turned outward, the neck is thick and short, and the belly is round and bulging, flowing upward. The shoulder is decorated with a flat handle. The handle has a corresponding hole near the mouth and the lid, which can be tied with a rope. The carcass is white and delicate, the glaze is bright, and the white is shining blue, with thin slices. It is elegant and exquisite, being called a boutique.

宋代,武义盛行饮茶之风,文人学士喜欢品茶玩味,把盏谈文,因此留下了许多脍炙人口的茶诗。这件青白瓷执壶,或许正是当年某位文人以茶会友、吟诗作赋时所用之物。

In the Song Dynasty, the tea-drinking prevailed in Wuyi. Scholars liked to taste and appreciate tea, leaving many popular poems on tea. This bluish white glazed porcelain pot may be exactly what a literati used when he met friends, drinking tea and chanting poems.

3. 南宋徐谓礼文书
Documentary archives of Xu Weili, the Southern Song Dynasty

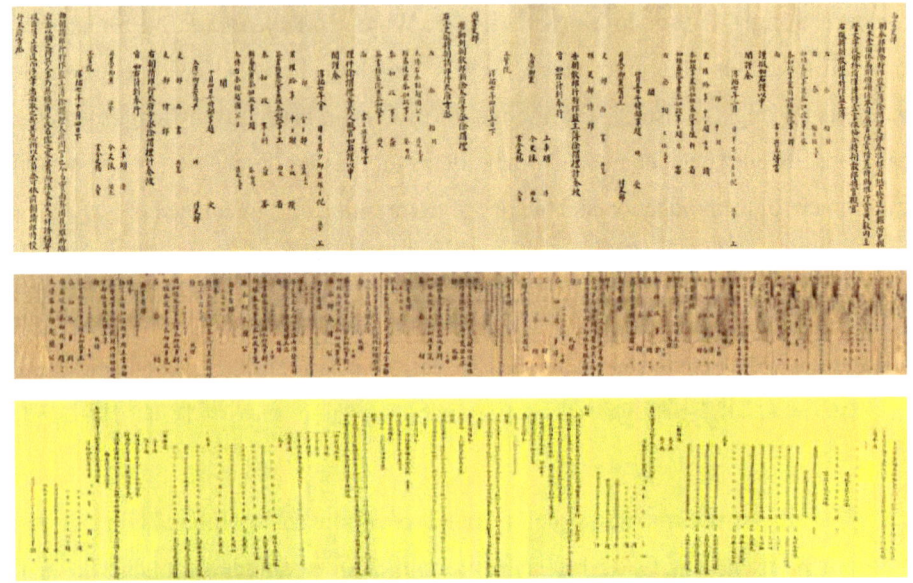

文书共17卷，总长3 220厘米，宽39厘米，载文4万余字。

It has a total of 17 volumes, with a total length of 3,220 cm, a width of 39 cm, and more than 40,000 Chinese characters.

南宋徐谓礼文书系国家一级珍贵文物，是迄今为止国内出土的最为系统的一部宋代纸质文书。徐谓礼文书由告身、敕黄、印纸三部分构成，完整地记录其从嘉定十四年到淳祐十二年近三十年的仕宦履历，真实地反映了南宋文官制度和政务运作情况，具有重要的文物价值和学术意义。尤其是印纸，此前只见于宋代文献记载，此次乃首次得见实物，其内容十分丰富，是我国独一无二的瑰宝。

The documentary archives of Xu Weili of the Southern Song Dynasty is Class A heritage under national protection. It is the most systematic Song Dynasty paper document unearthed in China so far. Xu Weili documentary archives compose of three parts: *gaoshen* (letter of appointment), *chihuang* (letter of commission) and *yinzhi* (performance document and performance evaluation form). It fully records his official career of nearly 30 years from the 14th year of Jiading to the 12th year of Chunyou, which truly reflects the civil service system and government operation in the Southern Song Dynasty, presenting important cultural relic value and academic significance. Especially *yinzhi*, which was only seen in the Song Dynasty literature before, was seen at first as a real object. It is rich in content, a unique treasure in our country.

录白：古代官员为存底的需要，将"告身""敕黄"和"印纸"等代表个人身份的官文书，依照原文格式抄录副本，称为"录白"，即文书原件的复制本。徐谓礼文书，就是随葬的"录白"副本。

Lubai: in order to keep the records, the ancient officials copied the official documents representing personal identities such as *gaoshen*, *chihuang* and *yinzhi* in the original format, being called *lubai*. It is the copy of the original document. Xu Weili documentary archives are the funeral copy of *lubai*.

告身：官员身份的主要凭证。宋代职官，由寄禄官（阶官）和差遣（实际职务）两部分组成。告身主要是阶官的"任命状"，即朝廷授予官员寄禄官的身份证书，略似于现在干部的行政级别证书。

Gaoshen: it is the main proof of the official identity. The officials in the Song Dynasty consisted of two parts: *jiluguan* (official rank) and *chaiqian* (actual position). Gaoshen mainly is the letter of appointment of official rank, namely, is the identity certificate granted by the court to the official. It is similar to the administrative rank certificate of cadres today.

敕黄：官员差遣（实际职务）的委任状。敕，自上告下之词；黄，用黄色绫纸书写，合称"敕黄"。敕黄由中书省拟定、审核，尚书省实施，并以皇帝制敕的名义签发。

Chihuang: it is the letter of commission of official *chaiqian* (actual position). *chi* means commanding words from the court and *huang* means these words were written on yellow flint paper, and then collectively called "*chihuang*". It was drafted and reviewed by Zhongshusheng (similar to today's the State Council), implemented by Shangshusheng (similar to the top ministry), and issued in the name of the emperor.

印纸：官员的档案记录与"绩效考核表"。官员上任，上级部门颁发一份印纸与其相随。将官员在任内的作为和表现记录在档案内，称"批书"，作为日后考核、升迁的依据。此前，印纸只见于宋代文献记载，徐谓礼文书出土后首次得见实物。

Yinzhi: it is the official's performance document and performance evaluation form. When the official takes office, the higher-level department issues *yinzhi* to record his deeds and performances during their tenure, which is called *pishu* as the basis for future evaluation and promotion. *yinzhi*, which was only seen in the Song Dynasty literature before, was seen at first as a real object.

中国宋史研究会原会长、国务院参事、北京大学教授邓小南认为，徐谓礼文书填补了宋史研究的空白，将对宋史研究产生深远的影响，其意义非凡。史学大师陈寅恪先生有云："华夏民族之文化，历数千载之演进，造极于赵宋之世。"南宋一朝的典章制度、思想文化，灿然可观，影响深远。徐谓礼文书揭示的文官政治，是南宋典章制度的核心，其凝聚了古人治国理政的经验和智慧，有待于人们进一步发掘、研究和利用。

Deng Xiaonan, former president of the Chinese Society of Song History, Counselor of the State Council, and Professor of Peking University, believed that Xu Weili's documents filled the gaps in the study of Song history and would have a profound impact on the study of Song history. The historian Mr. Chen Yinke said, "The culture of the Chinese nation evolving over thousands of years reached the peak in the Song dynasty." The rule system, ideology and culture of the Southern Song Dynasty are splendid and impressive, leaving a far-reaching influence. The civil politics revealed in Xu Weili's documents is the core of the ruling system of the Southern Song Dynasty. The experience and wisdom of ancient people governing the country condensed in these documents need to be further explored, studied and used.

4. 新石器时代玉玦

Jade *jue* of the Neolithic Age

该器通长3.6厘米，厚0.8厘米。

Length: 3.6 cm; height: 0.8 cm.

5. 唐婺州窑青瓷褐斑瓶
Celadon vase with brown spots of Wuzhou kiln, the Tang Dynasty

该器口径7.3厘米，底径7.6厘米。

Top rim diameter: 7.3 cm; foot rim diameter: 7.6 cm.

6. 宋仿商云雷纹龙首耳四足铜簋
Copper vessel with four feet and patterns of clouds, lightning and a dragonhead in style of the Shang and the Song Dynasties

该器通长24.6厘米，通宽15.2厘米，通高21厘米。

Length: 24.6 cm; width: 15.2 cm; height: 21 cm.

7. 南宋龙泉窑青瓷双鱼洗

Celadon basin with patterns of double fish of Longquan kiln, the Southern Song Dynasty

该器口径12.6厘米，高2.9厘米。

Top rim diameter: 12.6 cm; height: 2.9 cm.

8. 南宋缠枝纹镂空金镯

Gold brace with hollowed pattern of intertwisted branches, the Southern Song Dynasty

该器直径7.3厘米，高0.8厘米。

Diameter: 7.3 cm; height: 0.8 cm.

9. 元龙泉窑青黄釉波纹口樽形花盆

Greenish-yellow flowerpot with wavy fringes of Longquan kiln, the Yuan Dynasty

该器口径10.6厘米，底径6.8厘米，高8.5厘米。

Top rim diameter: 10.6 cm; bottom rim diameter: 6.8 cm; height: 8.5 cm.

10. 明崇祯三年毛氏汲古阁刻本——欧阳修《五代史》

Block printed *History of the Five Dynasties* by Ouyang Xiu, the third year of Chongzhen of the Ming Dynasty

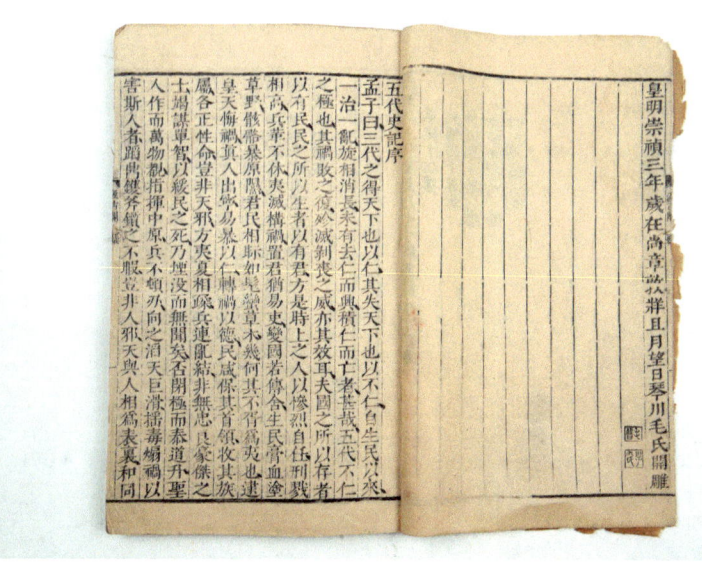

11. 清鹤蝠蝶三连镂空钟形流苏银吊坠

Silver bell-shaped pendent with patterns of crane, bat and butterfly and tassels, the Qing Dynasty

该器长19.6厘米，宽5.9厘米，厚0.8厘米。

Length: 19.6 cm; width: 5.9 cm; thickness: 0.8 cm.

武义县柳城畲族镇人民政府收藏。

It is collected in people's government of Shezu town in Liucheng, Wuyi County.

12. 清乾隆五十二年梅李来土地买卖契书

Converge of land transaction of Mei Lilai, in the 52nd year of Qianlong of the Qing Dynasty

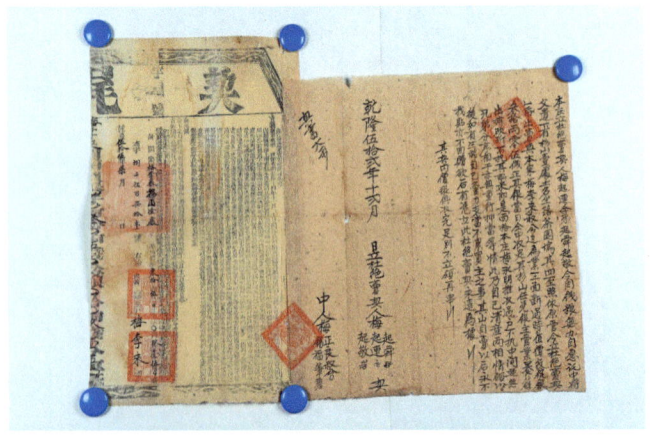

该书通长71.3厘米，高51.7厘米。

Length: 71.3 cm; height: 51.7 cm.

13. 清道光十九年佚名课会抄本

Transcript of lectures by anonym, the nineteenth year of Daoguang of the Qing Dynasty

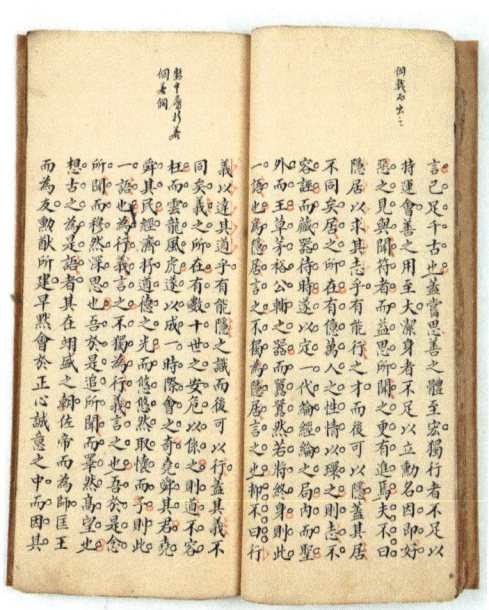

14. 清张曾扬白频红杏纸本行书对联

Couplets in semi-cursive script on red paper by Zhang Zengyang, the Qing Dynasty

该对联横31.8厘米，长128.5厘米。

Width: 31.8 cm; length:128.5 cm.

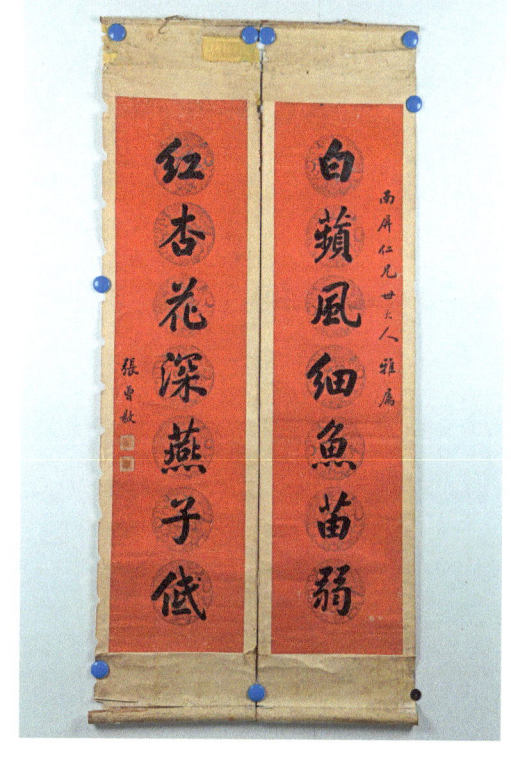

15. **清光绪俞锦云行书四壁满庭对联**

Couplets in semi-cursive script by Yu Jinyun, in Guangxu Period of the Qing Dynasty

该对联横31.5厘米，长134.2厘米。
Width: 31.5 cm; length: 134.2 cm.

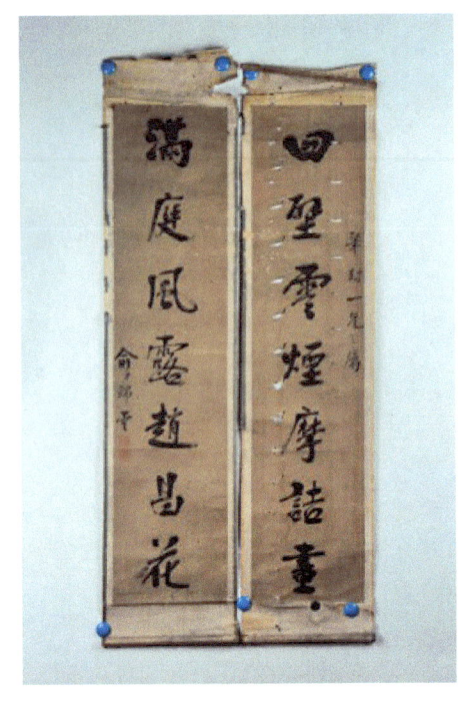

16. **清光绪丙午科千秋鉴浙江选取职卷**

List of Qianqiu Bureau of Zhejiang Province in 1906, Guangxu Period of the Qing Dynasty

17. 清光绪宣平县鳌峰书院俞成原课艺卷

Script of lectures of Aofeng School by Yu Chengyuan in Xuanping County, Guangxu Period of the Qing Dynasty

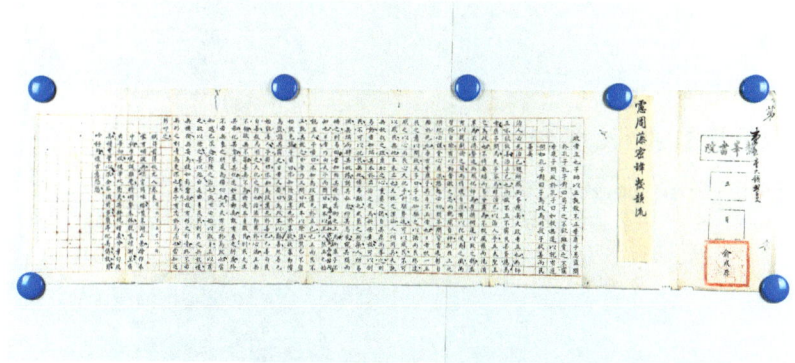

该作品横111.9厘米，长28.8厘米。

Width: 111.9 cm; length: 28.8 cm.

18. 民国时期朱光瘦骨筇支行书横幅

Horizontal scroll in semi-cursive script by Zhu Guang, the Republic of China (1912–1949)

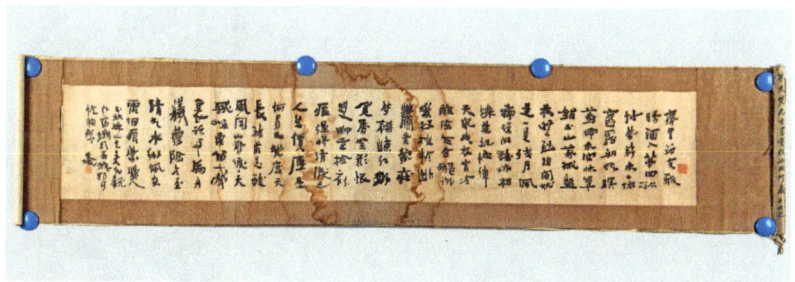

该作品横129.5厘米，长22.7厘米。

Width: 129.5 cm; length: 22.7 cm.

19. 民国十五年（1926年）朱伯行隶书其存左骖八言对联

Couplets in semi-clerical script by Zhu Bo, the Republic of China in 1926

该对联横31厘米，长121厘米。
Width: 31 cm; length: 121 cm.

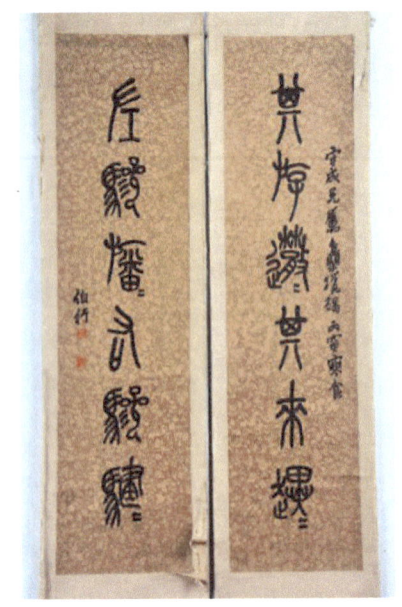

20. 1995年何海霞迎旭写意图轴

Scroll of painting of the lotus in sunrise by He Haixia, 1995

该作品横43.5厘米，长67.3厘米。
Width: 43.5 cm; length: 67.3 cm.

第十章 浦江博物馆
Pujiang Museum

1. 新石器时代上山文化大口盆
Big-mouth basin of Shangshan Culture in the Neolithic Age

该器口径44.8厘米，底径13.2厘米，高13.8厘米。

Top rim diameter: 44.8 cm; bottom rim diameter: 13.2 cm; height: 13.8 cm.

该器于浦江上山遗址出土。它为三角形唇，口沿向外翻卷，腹壁斜弧内收，平底，偶见底部微凹。外红胎黑的夹炭陶，胎质较薄，质地较坚硬，涂敷层较厚。内外壁均施红陶衣。原器物保存甚好，仅有局部复原，是上山文化中最为典型的出土文物。

It was unearthed at the Shangshan site of Pujiang. It has a triangular lip, with the edge of the mouth rolling outwards and the body wall obliquely arcing inward. It has a flat bottom, which occasionally slightly concave. The carbon-filled pottery with red outside and black skin has a thinner body, a harder texture and a thicker coating. The inner and outer walls are covered with red pottery coating. The original artifacts are very well preserved, only partially restored, and are the most typical unearthed cultural relics of the Shangshan culture.

2. 南宋银鎏金凤凰纹花头簪

Gilded silver hairpin with design of phoenix, the Southern Song Dynasty

该器通长17厘米，凤长10厘米，凤宽6厘米。

Length: 17 cm; length of the phoenix: 10 cm; width of the phoenix: 6 cm.

簪头为昂首振翅飞舞的凤与凰，颈上披羽飞扬；尾翼一卷曲一长直，以区分雌雄。长脚簪与簪首垂直安置。其造型生动，制作技艺精湛。

At the top of the hairpin, there is the phoenix dancing with its head up and its wings fluttering, as well as with feathers flying around its neck and the tail wing being curled or straight, to distinguish between male phoenix and female phoenix. The long-legged hairpin is placed perpendicular to the hairpin top, which is vividly styled and super skilled.

3. 清李维贤坐唱图横披
Horizontal scroll of painting of sitting singers by Li Weixian, the Qing Dynasty

该作品长63厘米，横109厘米。

Length: 63 cm; width: 109 cm.

该作品被浦江博物馆收藏。画中共有29个人物，包括演奏乐器者6人，大人、小孩等各种人物23人。画中人物形象生动，栩栩如生。此画真实描绘出当时浦江什锦班在厅堂中演唱的情景，从画中可窥见当时风靡已久的浦江乱弹的演出风貌。

It is collected in Pujiang Museum. There are a total of 29 figures in the painting, including 6 musical instrument players, 23 adults and children of various figures. The figures are vivid and lifelike. They truly depict the scene of the Pujiang Assortment singing in the hall at that time, which shows popular Pujiang Luantan at that time.

李维贤（1825—1907年），浦江县李源莲塘沿（今属黄宅镇）人。他擅长人物绘画，兼善山水、花鸟和狮虎绘画。清咸丰十一年（1861年），太平军侍王李世贤占领金华、兰溪和浦江。李维贤加入太平军，随军绘制龙虎旗、饰物与侍王府壁画等。太平军败绩后，他被囚于兰溪监狱，后被释放。后来，他隐名改姓，流寓他乡。同治十三年（1874年）始返故里，他从事泥塑、壁画和写真，有风俗画《坐唱图》等传世，并被收入《浦江县志》（浙江人民出版社1990年版）中。

Li Weixian (1825—1907), a native of Liyuan Liantangyan (now Huangzhai Town), Pujiang County, was good at painting figures, landscapes, flowers and birds as well as lions and tigers. In the eleventh year of Xianfeng in the Qing Dynasty (1861), Shiwang Li Shixian of the Taiping Army occupied Jinhua, Lanxi and Pujiang. Li Weixian joined the Taiping Army and accompanied the army to paint dragon and tiger flags, ornaments, and murals of the King Shi's Residence. After the defeat of the Taiping Army, he was imprisoned in Lanxi Prison. After being released, he changed his name and wandered away. In the thirteenth year of Tongzhi (1874), he began to return to his hometown and engaged in clay sculpture, mural painting, and portraiture. Some genre paintings such as *Sitting While Singing* were handed down and included in *The Annuals of Pujiang County* (Zhejiang People's Publishing House, 1990 edition).

4. 东汉"尚方"龙虎纹铜镜
Copper mirror with patterns of dragons and tigers, the Eastern Han Dynasty

该铜镜直径12.6厘米,厚0.7厘米。

Diameter: 12.6 cm; thickness: 0.7 cm.

5. 三国婺州窑青瓷双系筒式罐
Celadon bucket with double loops of Wuzhou kiln, the Three Kingdoms Period

该罐高16厘米,口径14.7厘米,底径11.1厘米。

Height: 16 cm; top rim diameter: 14.7 cm; bottom rim diameter: 11.1 cm.

6. 西晋婺州窑青瓷虎子
Celadon Huzi of Wuzhou kiln, the Western Jin Dynasty

该器高15.7厘米，腹围66厘米，底径14厘米。

Height: 15.7 cm; diameter of the belly rim: 66 cm; bottom rim diameter: 14 cm.

7. 唐海兽葡萄铜镜
Copper mirror with patterns of sea animals and grapes, the Tang Dynasty

该铜镜直径14.7厘米，厚1.1厘米。

Diameter: 14.7 cm; thickness: 1.1 cm.

8. 唐婺州窑青瓷鸡首壶
Celadon pot with decorations of chicken head of Wuzhou kiln, the Tang Dynasty

该壶高19厘米，口径6.1厘米，底径5.8厘米。

Height: 19 cm; top rim diameter: 6.1 cm; bottom rim diameter: 5.8 cm.

9. 唐箕形石砚
Dustpan shaped ink stone, the Tang Dynasty

该砚长18.6厘米，后宽10.3厘米，前宽11.9厘米，高3.7厘米。

Length: 18.6 cm; back width: 10.3 cm; front width: 11.9 cm; height: 3.7 cm.

10. 北宋婺州窑青瓷带盖多角瓶
Celadon covered vase with decoration of horns, the Northern Song Dynasty

该瓶通高27.3厘米，口径7.2厘米，底径8.1厘米。

Height: 27.3 cm; top rim diameter: 7.2 cm; bottom rim diameter: 8.1 cm.

11. 北宋青瓷缠枝花纹碗
Celadon bowl with patterns of vines, the Northern Song Dynasty

该碗高7.4厘米，口径18.6厘米，足径5.1厘米。

Height: 7.4 cm; top rim diameter: 18.6 cm; bottom rim diameter: 5.1 cm.

12. 北宋青瓷划花镂空枕
Celadon pillow with hollowed patterns, the Northern Song Dynasty

该瓷枕高13.5厘米，长18.3厘米，横24.3厘米。

Height: 13.5 cm; length: 18.3 cm; width: 24.3 cm.

13. 北宋錾鹦鹉纹圆形银盒
Round silver box with carved patterns of parrot, the Northern Song Dynasty

该盒通高5厘米，口径6.5厘米，底径4.8厘米。

Height: 5 cm; top rim diameter: 6.5 cm; bottom rim diameter: 4.8 cm.

14. 明龙泉窑青瓷粉盒
Celadon compact of Longquan kiln, the Ming Dynasty

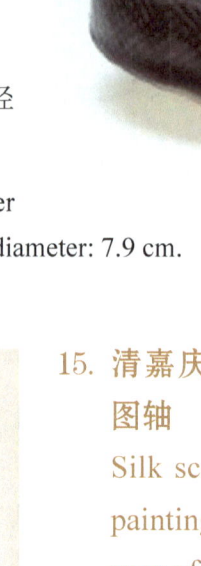

该盒通高4.9厘米，盖径8.2厘米，口径7.9厘米。

Height: 4.9 cm; diameter of the cover: 8.2 cm; top rim diameter: 7.9 cm.

15. 清嘉庆十六年司马钟绢本设色花鸟图轴
Silk scroll of colored flower-and-bird painting by Sima Zhong, the sixteenth year of Jiaqing, the Qing Dynasty

该作品长130厘米，横40厘米。

Length: 130 cm; width: 40 cm.

16. 清重印明万历六年刻本《金华府志》(三十卷)

Reprinted *Jin Hua Fu Zhi*, 30 volumes of published in the sixth year of Wanli Period of the Ming Dynasty, the Qing Dynasty

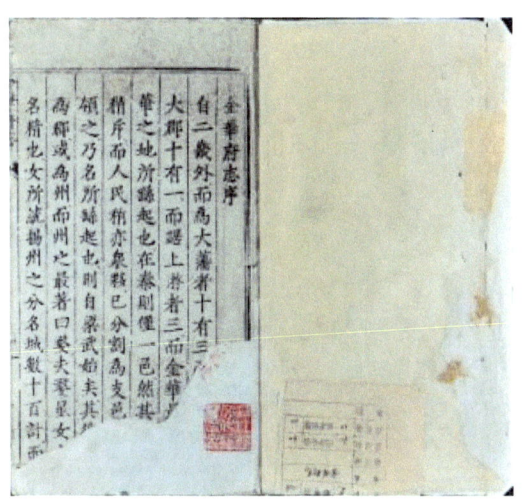

该作品通长29厘米，通宽17厘米，共10册。

Length: 29 cm; width: 17 cm; 10 books.

17. 清同治十三年浦江县张时上纸门牌

Paper doorplate of Zhang Shishang of Pujiang County, the thirteenth year of Tongzhi, the Qing Dynasty

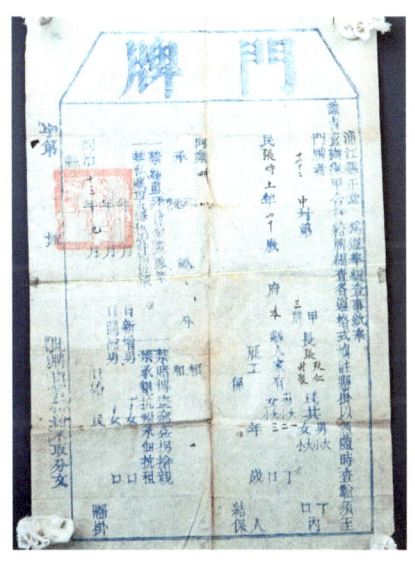

该门牌长46厘米，横31厘米。

Length: 46 cm; width: 31 cm.

18. 民国十三年（1924年）吴蒹之牡丹水仙图轴

Scroll of painting of peony and narcissus by Wu Fuzhi, the thirteenth year of the Republic of China (1924)

该作品长174厘米，横93.5厘米。

Length: 174 cm; width: 93.5 cm.

19. 民国十七年（1928年）郑祖纬抱琴图轴

Scroll of painting of a figure holding an instrument by Zheng Zuwei, the seventeenth year of the Republic of China (1928)

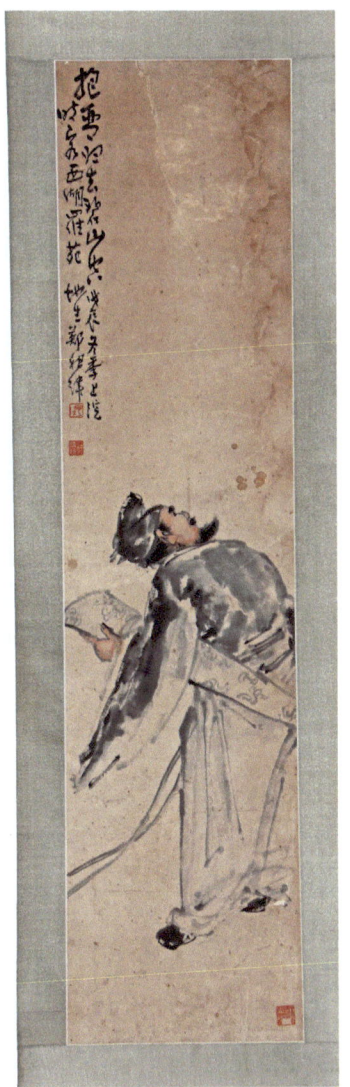

该作品长132厘米，横32厘米。

Length: 132 cm; width: 32 cm.

20. 1954年张书旂梅月图卷
Scroll of painting of plum and moon by Zhang Shuqi, 1954

该作品长102厘米,横52厘米。

Length: 102 cm; width: 52 cm.

21. 当代沙孟海行书"百花齐放 百家争鸣"横披

Horizontal scroll of semi-cursive script of "Bai Hua Qi Fang, Bai Jia Zheng Ming" by Sha Menghai, in modern times

该作品长130厘米,横64厘米。

Length: 130 cm; width: 64 cm.

第十一章　磐安县文物管理办公室
Office of Artifact Management of Pan'an County

1. 宋龙泉窑粉青釉小碗
Light greenish blue glazed bowl of Longquan kiln, the Song Dynasty

该碗高4.1厘米。

Height: 4.1 cm.

此碗为芒口，弧腹，圈足。内外壁均施粉青釉，釉色匀净、肥润，釉面开片。它是同时期龙泉窑中的精品。因口沿无釉，露出胎骨，故称"芒口"，往往因采用覆烧法所致。达官贵人在使用时，则多以金、银、铜镶器口，既可避其"芒"，亦可夸富。

It is deigned with *mangkou* (a kind of design that the mouth rim of the object is glazeless), with arc belly and circle feet. The light greenish blue glaze is applied to both the inner and outer walls. It is evenly glazed, rich and smooth. Big flakes of glaze are on the surface of the bowl. It is a fine product of Longquan Kiln in the same period. The rim of the mouth is not glazed and the fetal bone is exposed, which is called *"mangkou"*, caused by the over-firing method. When dignitaries use it, they usually use gold, silver, and copper to inlay the mouth rims, which can avoid the glazeless mouth and can also boast of wealth.

2. 南宋龙泉窑粉青釉三足炉
Celadon stove with three feet of Longquan kiln, the Southern Song Dynasty

该炉高11.4厘米。
Height: 11.4 cm.

磐安安文镇半月山宋墓出土。高11.4厘米，长轴12.9厘米，短轴12.3厘米，内口径10.60厘米，底径5.2厘米，椭圆形。圆唇弧腹略收，双耳中有圆孔，三足中空似葱管。胎质洁白，釉色粉青，光泽柔和淡雅，釉层均匀。外表底部稍薄，一足小残。

It was unearthed from a Song tomb of Banyue Mountain in Anwen Town, Pan'an. The height is 11.4 cm, the long axis is 12.9 cm, the short axis is 12.3 cm, the inner top rim diameter is 10.60 cm, and the bottom rim diameter is 5.2 cm. It is oval, with round lip and arc belly, and with holes in its double ears and with three feet hollow like scallion tubes. The fetus is pure white, and the glaze is light greenish blue. It is evenly glazed, being soft and elegant. The bottom of the exterior is slightly thin, with a slight broken feet.

3. 东汉原始瓷盘口壶
Pot with broad rim, the Eastern Han Dynasty

该壶高24.8厘米。

Height: 24.8 cm.

4. 汉铁鼎
Iron tripod, the Han Dynasty

该鼎高29.8厘米。

Height: 29.8 cm.

5. 西晋青瓷碗
Celadon bowl, the Western Jin Dynasty

该碗高6厘米。

Height: 6 cm.

6. 东晋青瓷双系盘口壶
Celadon pot with two loops, the Eastern Jin Dynasty

该壶高32.2厘米。

Height: 32.2 cm.

7. 南朝青瓷砚
Celadon ink stone, the Southern Dynasty

该砚高5.5厘米。

Height: 5.5 cm.

8. 南朝青瓷盘口壶

Celadon pot with broad rim, the Southern Dynasty

该壶高36.7厘米。

Height: 36.7 cm.

9. 南朝青瓷槅

Celadon lattice, the Southern Dynasty

该器高3.8厘米。

Height: 3.8 cm.

10. **唐青瓷罐**
    Celadon Pot, the Tang Dynasty

    该罐高37.6厘米。
    Height: 37.6 cm.

11. **唐青瓷谷仓**
    Celadon granary, the Tang Dynasty

    该器高38.5厘米。
    Height: 38.5 cm.

12. **宋青瓷多角瓶**

    Celadon pot with decorations of horns, the Song Dynasty

    该瓶高38厘米。
    Height: 38 cm.

13. **宋青瓷多角瓶**

    Celadon pot with decorations of horns, the Song Dynasty

    该瓶高52厘米。
    Height: 52 cm.

14. 宋青瓷盘龙瓶
Celadon vase with design of dragon, the Song Dynasty

该瓶高43.7厘米。
Height: 43.7 cm.

15. 宋云水纹青铜镜
Bronze mirror with patterns of water waves, the Song Dynasty

该铜镜长15.2厘米，宽9.6厘米，厚0.6厘米。
Length: 15.2 cm; width: 9.6 cm; thickness: 0.6 cm.

16. 宋带柄青铜镜

Bronze mirror with a handle, the Song Dynasty

该铜镜长21.9厘米，宽12.4厘米，厚0.3厘米。

Length: 21.9 cm; width: 12.4 cm; thickness: 0.3 cm.

17. 元龙泉窑青瓷碗

Celadon bowl of Longquan kiln, the Yuan Dynasty

该碗高4厘米。

Height: 4 cm.

18. 清珍珠釉蟾蜍

Pearl covered toad, the Qing Dynasty

该器长26.5厘米，宽19.5厘米，高13.4厘米。

Length: 26.5 cm; width: 19.5 cm; height: 13.4 cm.

19. 现代党徽刻石

Stone engraved with emblem of CPC, in modern times

该石长48厘米，宽42厘米，高26厘米。

Length: 48 cm; width: 42 cm; height: 26 cm.

第三部分

难字阐析

Part 3
Interpretation of Difficult Words

第十二章　八婺古韵
——金华市博物馆历史文化陈列展览难字解读
The Ancient Bawu:
Interpretation of Difficult Words Displayed in the Historical and Cultural Exhibition of Jinhua Museum

一、万年上山——史前时期的金华
Shangshan Culture of Tens of Thousands of Years: The Prehistoric Jinhua

1. 展品
Exhibits

新石器时代石镞
The Neolithic stone arrowheads

镞（zú）：箭头。（石镞）
Zú: The arrow. (Shi Zu, stone arrowheads)

新石器时代石钺
The Neolithic Shi Yue

钺（yuè）：古代兵器名，形状像斧。（石钺）

Yuè: Name of an ancient weapon, shaped as an axe. (Shi Yue, a battle-axe used in ancient China)

新石器时代石锛
The Neolithic Shi Ben

锛（bēn）：锛子，削平木料的一种工具，用时向下向内用力。（石锛）

Bēn: The adze, a tool for slicing off woods, used with a downward inward force. (Shi Ben)

2. 展板
Exhibition Board

圜（huán）：两个读音，huán，围绕；yuán，同"圆"。

Huán: It has two pronunciations, one for huán with a meaning of "surrounding", the other for yuán with a meaning of "a circle".

耜（sì）：古代的一种农具，形状如锹，用于翻土。（用耜翻耕和平整土地）

Sì: An ancient farm implement, shaped as a shovel, used for turning the soil. (Plowing and leveling the land with Si)

崧（sōng）：同"嵩""高"。（崧泽文化）

Sōng: The same as "lofty" and "high". (Songze Culture)

二、於越姑蔑——先秦时期的金华
States of Wuyue and Gumie: Jinhua in the Pre-Qin Period

1. 展品
Exhibits

东汉网格纹陶罍
The cobwebbing pottery jar in the Eastern Han Dynasty

罍（léi）：盛酒水的器皿。（网纹陶罍）

Léi: A wine container. (a cobwebbing pottery jar)

商代云纹铜铙
Bronze clouding pattern Nao in the Shang Dynasty

铙（náo）：军中乐器，像铃铛，中间没有舌。（青铜云纹铙）

Náo: A ball-like military instrument without a metal ball in the middle. (Bronze clouding Nao)

宋铜矢镞
The bronze arrowhead in the Song Dynasty

镞（zú）：箭头。（青铜箭镞）

Zú: An arrow. (Bronze arrowheads)

2. 展板
Exhibition Board

於（wū）：文言叹词。（地名：於越）

Wū: A Classical Chinese interjection. (Name of a place: Wu Yue)

鄞（yín）：古地名，春秋时属越，即今浙江省鄞县。（鄞州区）

Yín: Name of an ancient place, belonging to Yue during the Spring and Autumn Period, the present Yin county in Zhejiang. (Yinzhou District）

句（gōu）：姓氏"勾"。勾又写作"句"。

Gōu: Family name. Also written as "句" (Ju).

蔑（mie）：姑蔑，地名。

Mie: Gu Mie, Name of a place.

觿（xī）：古代一种解结的锥子，用骨、玉等制成，也用作佩饰。

Xī: An awl for untying the knot in ancient times, made of bones and jades, also used as an accessory.

玦（jué）：环形有缺口的佩玉。

Jué: Jade in ring shape, with a breach.

三、婺州初兴——秦汉六朝时期的金华
The Preparatory Rising of Wuzhou: Jinhua in the Qin and Han Dynasties and Six Dynasties

1. 展品
Exhibits

西晋青瓷灶

Celadon stove in the Western Jin Dynasty

甑（zèng）：古代的一种炊具，底部有许多小孔，放在鬲（lì）上蒸食物。（一甑二釜陶灶）

Zèng: An ancient cooking utensil, with multiple holes in the bottom, used for steaming food on Li (an ancient cooking tripod with hollow legs). (A steamer with two pottery kettles)

东晋青瓷双系盂
The double green glazed porcelain jar in the Eastern Jin Dynasty

盂（yú）：一种盛液体的器皿。（青瓷双系盂）

Yú: A vessel for holding liquid. (Double green glazed porcelain jar)

南朝青瓷钵
The celadon bowl in the Southern Dynasties

钵（bō）：洗涤或盛放东西的陶制器具。（青瓷钵）

Bō: A ceramic utensil used to wash or hold something. (celadon bowl)

2. 展板
Exhibition Board

苌（cháng）:（1）古书上说的一种植物；（2）姓。（人名：龙丘苌）

Cháng: (1) a kind of plant recorded in ancient books; (2) a family name. (Name of a person: Long Qiuchang)

瀫（gǔ）：瀫水，现在的衢江。

Gǔ: Gu Shui, the present Qujiang.

碓（duì）：一种木石做成的捣米器具，舂（chōng）米的作坊。（水碓）

Duì: A utensil consisting of wood and stone to husk rice, or a rice-husking workshop. (*Shui Dui:* rice-husking device powered by water)

翕（xī）：合，聚，和顺。（人名：傅翕）

Xī: United, being together, being peaceful. (Name of a person Fu Xi)

四、千古风流——隋唐宋元时期的金华
A Blossoming Wuzhou: Jinhua in the Sui, Tang, Song and Yuan Dynasties

1. 展品
Exhibits

乳浊釉鬲式炉

Opacified Glaze-typed Li furnace

鬲（lì）：一种古代炊具，形状像鼎而足部中空。

Lì: An ancient Ding-shaped cooking utensil whose legs are hollow.

北宋鎏金观音铜坐像（仿）

The seated statue of Gilded copper Guanyin in the Northern Song Dynasty (Imitation)

鎏（liú）：成色好的黄金。（银鎏金钗，鎏金铜水月观音造像）

Liú: Fine gold. (silver-gilded nobile, gilded bronze water-moon Guanyin statue)

宋螭龙纹青白玉璧

The bluish-white dragon-pattern jade in the Song Dynasty

螭（chī）：古代传说中一种没有角的龙。古建筑或器物、工艺品上常用它的形状作装饰。（螭龙纹青白玉璧）

Chī: A dragon without horns in the ancient legend, whose images were usually used to decorate ancient buildings, implements or art ware. (the bluish-white dragon-pattern jade)

2. 展板

Exhibition Board

旌（jīng）：古代用羽毛装饰的旗子，又指普通的旗子。（旌孝门）

Jīng: An ancient flag decorated with feathers, or usually a common flag. (Jingxiao Gate)

矶（jī）：江边突出的岩石或小石山。（石矶岩）

Jī: Rocks or small rock hills protruding the riverside. (Shi Ji Yan)

谯（qiáo）：古代城门上建的楼，可以瞭望。（谯楼）

Qiáo: A construction built on the ancient city gate from which one can keep a lookout. (Qiao Lou)

炀（yáng）：古代谥法，去礼远众称"炀"。（隋炀帝）

Yáng: Rules for ancient posthumous titling, being away from rites and people. (the Emperor Yang of the Sui Dynasty)

曌（zhào）：同"照"，中国唐代武则天为自己名字造的字。（讨武曌檄文）

Zhào: Same as "照 (zhao)", created by the Empress Wu Zetian for her own in the Tang Dynasty. (An Essay against Wuzhao)

嗣（sì）：年号。（唐嗣圣元年）

Sì: Reign title. (the First year of Tang dynasty)

镠（líu）：人名。（钱镠）

Líu: Name of a person. (Qian Liu)

畿（jī）：古代称靠近国都的地方。（京畿）

Jī: A place close to the capital in ancient times. (Jing Ji)

擢（zhuó）：提拔，提升。（叶衡被擢为枢密院使）

Zhuó: To promote. (Ye Heng was promoted as the emissary of Privy Council)

鳜（guì）：一种体侧扁、性凶猛，生活在淡水中的鱼，味鲜美。它是一种中国特产，亦作"桂鱼"，有些地区称"花鲫鱼"。（桃花流水鳜鱼肥）

Guì: A kind of fish being flat and ferocious lives in freshwater. It is living in China and tastes delicious for cooking. It has an alternative name of "Gui Yu" or "Hua Jiyu" in some places. (Over peach-mirrored stream, where mandarin fish are full-grown.)

箬笠（ruò lì）：用箬竹叶及篾编成的宽边帽。（青箬笠，绿蓑衣，斜风细雨不须归。）

Ruò lì: A wide-brimmed hat compiled by Indocalamus leaves. (In my blue bamboo hat and green straw cloak, I'd fain go fishing careless of slanting wind and fine rain.)

五、八婺兴盛——明清时期的金华
A Prosperous Bawu: Jinhua in the Ming and Qing Dynasties

1. 展品
Exhibits

皋（gāo）：金华名僧，字心越，别号东皋。（东皋心越）

Gāo: A famous monk in Jinhua with a courtesy name of Xinyue and a pseudonym of Donggao. (Dong Gao Xin Yue)

佾（yì）：古代乐舞的行列。（佾庭）

Yì: Rows of ancient music and dance. (Yi Ting)

2. 展板
Exhibition Board

椁（guǒ）：棺材外面套的大棺材。（明代范氏石椁墓）

Guǒ: A large casket used to cover the coffin. (the stone coffin of the Fan family in the Ming Dynasty)

佥（qiān）：辅，辅助。（都指挥佥事）

Qiān: To assist. (General command aide)

倭寇（wō kòu）：元末到明中叶多次在朝鲜和我国沿海抢劫骚扰的日本强盗。

Wō kòu: Refer to Japanese robbers who constantly robbed and harassed coastal areas of China and Korea from the end of Yuan Dynasty to the middle of Ming Dynasty.

鞑靼（dá dá）：古代对北方游牧民族的称呼。

Dá dá: The ancient name of a nomadic people in the North of China.

戍（shù）：军队防守，戍边。

Shù: The military defense, guarding the frontiers or border regions.

茔（yíng）：坟墓，坟地。（坟茔）

Yíng: Grave, Cemetery. (Fen Ying: tomb)

溍（jìn）:（1）水名；（2）水貌。（黄溍，人名）

Jìn: (1) name of waters; (2) waterform. (The name of a person: Huang Jin)

巽（xùn）:（1）八卦之一，代表风；（2）古同"逊"，意为谦让恭顺。（称呼：九世祖巽源公）

Xùn: (1) One of the Eight Diagrams, representing the wind; (2) Same as "逊" with a meaning of humility in ancient times. (addressing: the ninth generation Xun Yuan Gong)

橐（tuó）：口袋，如负书担橐。（橐金而归）

Tuó: Pocket, Fu Shu Dan Tuo: carrying book case and luggage. (Tuo Jin Er Gui: Coming back home with gold)

饬（chì）：古同"敕"，意为告诫、命令。（谕饬）

Chì: Same as "敕", with a meaning of warning and ordering. (Yu Chi: official orders)

六、百年沧桑——近代时期的金华
Changes in Hardships: Jinhua in Modern Times

1. 展品
Exhibits

湜（shí）：形容水清见底。（人名，万湜思）

Shí: To describe clear water, which is so clear, that one can see down to the bottom. (The name of a person, Wan Shisi)

2. 展板
Exhibition Board

赣（gàn）：中国江西省的别称。

Gàn: The alternative name for Jiangxi Province in China.

第十三章　神奇大地
——金华地质文化陈列展览难字解读

Land of Wonders:
Interpretation of Difficult Words Displayed in Jinhua Geological Cultural Exhibition

垩（è）：白垩纪是地质年代中中生代的最后一个纪，始于公元前1.45亿年，结束于公元前6 500万年，历经8 000万年，是显生宙最长的一个阶段。

È: The Cretaceous Period, the last period of the Mesozoic in the geological age which starts from 145 million BC, and ends at 65 million BC. It lasts 80 million years and is the longest stage of the Phanerozoic.

喀（kā）：喀斯特地貌，以双龙洞为代表，具有溶蚀力的水对可溶性岩石（大多为石灰岩）进行溶蚀作用等所形成的地表和地下形态的总称，又称岩溶地貌。

Kā: The karst landform, represented by the Double Dragon Cave, is the generic term for ground surface and underground forms formed by erosion effect of water with dissolution force on soluble rock (mostly limestone), also called as Karst landform.

喙（huì）：嘴，特指鸟兽的嘴。（喙嘴龙类）

Huì: The beak, especially refers to the birds' beak. (Rhamphorhyn-choids)

钼（mù）：一种金属元素，可用来生产特种钢，是电子工业的重要材料。（钼矿）

Mù: A metallic element, the important materials in the electronic industry, used to produce special steel. (Mukuang: molybdenum minerals)

槠（zhū）：一种常绿乔木，叶长椭圆形，花黄绿色，果实球形；木材坚硬，可制器具。（甜槠）

Zhū: An evergreen tree, with oblong leaves, yellowish-green flowers and spherical fruits. It can be made into implements for its hard wood. (Tianzhu: Castanopsis eyrei)

栎（lì）：一种落叶乔木，叶长椭圆形，结球形坚果，叶可喂蚕；木材坚硬，可制家具，供建筑用，树皮可鞣皮或做染料。它亦称"麻栎""橡"，通称"柞树"。

Lì: A deciduous tree, with oblong leaves and spherical nuts. Its leaves are food for silkworm; it can be made into furniture and used in architecture for its hard wood. Its bark can be used as tanbark or dyestuff. It's also called as "German oak" "oak" and has a generic term for "bristle tooth oak".

栲（kǎo）：一种常绿乔木，叶长圆状披针形，果实球形，有短刺；木材坚硬，可做船橹、轮轴等。树皮含鞣酸，可制栲胶，又可制染料。

Kǎo: An evergreen tree, with oblong lancelet leaves, and spherical fruits with short spines on it. It can be made into boat oar and wheel axle for its hard wood. The tannic acid contained in the bark can be made into tannin extract and dyestuff.

榈（lǘ）：木名，紫红色，似紫檀，有花纹；性坚硬，可做器具或扇骨。（花榈木）

Lǘ: Name of wood, in fuchsia color, like the red sandalwood, with decorative pattern. It can be made into apparatus or fan ribs for its hard wood. (Hua lv Mu: rosewood)

蜓（tíng）：一种古代无脊椎动物，形状多样。最常见的呈纺锤形，壳小，大部分为石灰质。它最早出现在石炭纪，到二迭纪末期灭绝，是划分这两个地层的标准化石之一。

Tíng : An ancient invertebrate in various forms. The most common form is as fusiform with small shell most of which are calcareous infarct. It first showed up at Carboniferous period and became extinct at the late Permian period. It is one of the standard fossils to distinguish the two stratums.

氡（dōng）：一种气体元素，有放射性，无色无臭，不易跟其他元素化合。医药上用来治疗癌症。

Dōng: A kind of gas element with radioactivity, colorless and odorless, difficult to combine with other elements. It is used to cure cancer in medicine.

氟（fú）：一种气体元素，淡黄色，味臭、性毒。液态氟可作火箭燃料的氧化剂。含氟塑料和含氟橡胶有特别优良的性能。

Fú: A kind of gas element in light yellow, with odor and toxin. The liquid fluorine can be used as an oxidizer for rocket fuel. Both the fluorine plastic and fluorine rubber have excellent performances.

玢（bīn）:（1）一种玉的花纹；（2）火成岩的一种，例如，玢岩。

Bīn: (1) a jade pattern; (2) a kind of igneous rocks: Bin rock.

玢（fēn）：玻璃纸的一种，无色透明，有光泽，例如赛璐玢。

Fēn: a kind of cellophane, colorless, transparent and lustrous: Sailu Bin.

第十四章　乡土民风
——金华文化遗产陈列展览难字解读

Folk Customs:

Interpretation of Difficult Words Displayed in Jinhua Cultural Heritage Exhibition

涞（lái）：敬一涞，五世祖俞涞辈分排名敬一。

Lái : Jing Yilai, ranked as Jing Yi in the seniority in the fifth generation of Yulai family.

洧（wěi）：郑洧，人名。

Wěi : Zheng Wei, name of a person.

赆（jìn）：临别时赠送给远行人的路费、礼物。（赆仪钱）

Jìn: A gift or travelling expenses for a person who is going for a long journey at parting. (Jin Yi Qian: farewell money)

飨（xiǎng）：用酒食招待客人，泛指请人受用。（祭飨）

Xiǎng: To entertain guests with food and wine, generally refers to invite people to enjoy the meal. (Ji Xiang: to entertain guests with food and wine on mourning ceremonies)

庑（wǔ）：堂下周围的走廊、廊屋。（廊庑）

Wǔ: The corridors and galleries around the hall. (Lang Wu)

铳（chòng）：旧时指枪一类的火器。（火铳）

Chòng: Refers to firearms such as gun in old times. (Huo Chong)

蠹（dù）:(1) 蛀蚀器物的虫子：蠹虫。(2) 蛀蚀：流水不腐，户枢不蠹。

Dù: (1) a worm, which corrodes utensils: Du Chong. (2) erode: running water does not stink, frequently running door hinge does not suffer from worm biting.

第十五章　百工之乡
——金华工商文化陈列展览难字解读

Land of Handicrafts:
Interpretation of Difficult Words Displayed in Jinhua Industrial and Commercial Cultural Exhibition

癞痢（là lì）：俗称"秃疮"或"癞痢头"。（癞痢松）

Là lì: Commonly known as favas of the scalp or La Li head. (La Li Song)

亟（jí）：急切。（亟待解决的难题）

Jí: Urgent. (difficulties needed to be solved urgently)

衽（rèn）：同"衽"，古代睡觉时用的席子。（谁将登衽席）

Rèn: Same as "Ren (sleeping mat)", a mat used for sleeping in ancient times. (Who would be sitting on the Ren Xi? —— a sentence from a poem)

穋（lù）：后种先熟的谷类。（黄穋稻）

Lù: The grain crops, which were planted last but ripened first. (Huang Lu Dao)

榧（fěi）：一种常绿乔木，种子有很硬的壳，两端尖，称"榧子"；仁可食，亦可入药、榨油；木质坚硬，可做建筑材料。其通称"香榧"。（榧树）

Fěi: An evergreen tree. Its seeds, with very hard shells and sharp at both ends, are called as "Feizi". The kernel is edible and can be used as medicine and to extract oil. It can be used as construction material for its hard wood. It is generally called as "Xiang Fei". (Fei Shu)

苎（zhù）：一种多年生草本植物，茎皮含纤维质很多，是纺织工业的重要原料。（苎麻）

Zhù: The herbaceous perennial, rich in fibers at the stem bark, is an important material for textile industry. (Zhu Ma: ramie)

邑（yì）：城市，都城。（邑皆瓦屋）

Yì: City, Capital. (Yi Jie Wa Wu: the city is filled with tile houses)

埴（zhí）：黏土。（砖埴）

Zhí: Clay. (Zhuan Zhi, Clay brick)

瓴（fǎng）：瓶。（陶瓴）

Fǎng: Bottle. (Tao Fang)

鬻（yù）：卖，例如鬻歌、鬻画、鬻文为生、卖儿鬻女。（鬻技术于他乡）

Yù: Sell: Yu Ge, sing for money. Yu Hua, sell the paints. Yu Wen, make a living by writing. Mai Er Yu Nv, sell sons and daughters for money. (Yu skill, make a living on craftsmanship in other places)

篾（miè）：劈成条的竹片，亦泛指劈成条的芦苇、高粱秆皮等。（篾匠）

Miè: Sliced bamboo, also generally refers to sliced reed and sorghum stalk skins. (Mie Jiang: craftsman)

黍（shǔ）：一种一年生草本植物，叶线形，子实淡黄色，去皮后称黄米，比小米稍大，煮熟后有黏性。（其蔗似黍）

Shǔ: An annual herb, with linear leaves and light yellow fruits, is called as yellow rice after husking, slightly bigger than millet, sticky after being cooked thoroughly. (Qi Zhe Si Shu: Shu is sweet as sugar cane)

啖（dàn）：吃或给人吃。（杆可啖）

Dàn: To eat or to feed others. (Gan Ke Dan: the rod is edible)

啻（chì）：止，仅仅。（不啻数千人）

Chì: Only. (Bu Chi Shu Qian Ren: more than thousands of people)